The
Goddess
in the
Office

Dear
Mona,
Congratulations
on your new job!
You are a goddess!
Love,
Karen

Also by Zsuzsanna E. Budapest

The Grandmother of Time
The Holy Book of Women's Mysteries
Grandmother Moon

The Goddess in the Office

A Personal Energy Guide
for the Spiritual Warrior at Work

Zsuzsanna E. Budapest

HarperSanFrancisco
A Division of HarperCollins*Publishers*

Illustrations by Anneli S. Rufus. Design by Katherine Tillotson.

FIRST EDITION

Library of Congress Cataloging-in-Publication Data
Budapest, Zsuzsanna Emese, 1940–
    The goddess in the office : a personal energy guide for the
  spiritual warrior at work / Zsuzsanna Budapest. — 1st ed.
      p. cm.
  Includes bibliographical references.
  ISBN 0-06-250087-2 (alk. paper)
  1. Self-actualization (Psychology).   2. Gaia hypothesis.
3. Meditation. 4. Ecofeminism. I. Title.
BF637.S4B83 1993
131—dc20
                                            91-58920
                                                  CIP

93   94   95   96   97 ❖ MAL 10 9 8 7 6 5 4 3

This edition is printed on acid-free paper that meets the
American National Standards Institute Z39.48 Standard.

This book is dedicated respectfully and gratefully to

Professor Anita Hill
Dr. Francis Conley
And the millions of women who tell the truth.

Acknowledgments

I would like to thank my working woman friends, Brenda, Cathlyn, Diana, Hilary, Jacqueline, Janet, Laurel, Leslie, Marcy, Margaret, Mary Lou, and Shannon, who have given me the opportunity to work out problems for this special magical book for the workplace. My deep thanks to Diana Paxson, my magical editor, without whom I could not finish any work with confidence. Thanks also to my Harper editor, Barbara Moulton, for giving me an honest appraisal. I always find her insights powerful. My deep thanks to professor Anita Hill and Dr. Francis Conley, who made me mad enough to write down my searing spells against sexual harassment.

Beware! After this book the office will never be the same. Thank the Goddess!

Introduction

Hurray for the working woman, because you have resisted propaganda against your own interest, and you don't get scared when you are told that having a life and a job will be too much for you. You don't cave in when the media tries to make you wear uncomfortable clothes in the name of fabricated femininity. You buy clothes that are comfortable and define femininity according to your own needs.

Hurray for you, working sister, because when they told you to stay away from feminism, you embraced its principles and called it whatever was safe at the time. And more praises upon you, because when those doors of opportunity finally opened, you bravely marched right through and kept them open for the women who followed you. Hurray for you, working woman, because you started humanizing the workplace and began speaking out against sexual harassment. You demanded flexible hours, child care, and maternity care for both you and your spouse.

Equality needs examples, and it is you, my most respected one, who will be the conquering hera when this century is through. Do not despair if the courts do not protect you. It is the terrible backlash against your awesome effectiveness that is raging now. But never has history gone backward, and never have reactionaries been remembered by posterity. Who knows the names of men who fought against the women's vote? We only know and revere those women who worked for it. Your heras are working spirits: Elizabeth Cady Stanton, who a hundred years ago fought for your right to keep your own earnings; Susan B. Anthony, who tirelessly worked for your right to vote; and Alice Paul, who drafted the Equal Rights Amendment, which still is not law.

From sweatshops to child labor laws, you have fought your way painstakingly to every level of management and government, opening the minds of the collective consciousness to accept women as effective employees. You broke the ice! But you have not yet achieved your goal. The Information Age is upon us, and now is when you will go "all the way, baby." You already can see that some jobs go out of style, while others are born. The financial markets are changing; the need for your brain and brawn will be greater than the need to humiliate you and scare you back into low-paying jobs and servitude. You are now a true working majority. My blessings and respect to you, my working sister, and thank you for your perseverance and craft.

Who is the Goddess, and what is she doing in the office? To me, she is an expression of the spiritual power of all working women. She enables us to find personal and financial satisfaction, increase our work productivity, and defend ourselves and our jobs. She enhances our powers as women/mothers/managers/producers/leaders through a deeper understanding of the seven powers Mother Nature has given us. These seven powers relate to the seven days of the week. They are Monday, grounding; Tuesday, managing and using the will; Wednesday, developing better communication; Thursday, using the powers of the heart and love; Friday, managing and using one's feelings; Saturday, gaining new vision; and Sunday, using and uniting the powers of the spirit.

This book is your daily guide from Monday through Sunday. It is your personal energy guide to show you how to navigate through the week as a gentle spiritual warrior. Use your own intellect and embellish the suggested spells. Make them your own in order to enhance their effectiveness. Don't discuss the spells you cast with anybody who does not work them with you; let your secrecy be a vessel for its power. Witches believe that when you talk about a spell you are casting, you are "bleeding" it of power.

This book comes from the pen of a feminist witch to your hands. So for the first time in herstory you, my most respected ones, have access to Goddess magic in the workplace. Use it wisely and carefully. Enjoy your newfound power and remember that every time you make a choice, "Thou art Goddess!"

Zsuzsanna Budapest
May 5, 9992 A.D.A.
(After the Development of Agriculture)

Welcoming the Wild Woman

Wild Woman Comes to the Office

You have probably heard a lot about the wounded child within, the Goddess/God within, the animus and anima within, the ego and the id. It's pretty crowded in there! The Goddess within is a difficult image, because you search for this luminous perfect woman inside yourself, shining and omnipotent, and often you can't quite identify with her—she is too perfect. However, during my meditations I have encountered again and again a natural creature I call the Wild Woman. Perhaps she is a form of Artemis, the soul of the wild who roams through the woods as well as guiding the moon across the skies. Her image is inside our psyches for sure.

Wild Woman represents our bodies, our genetic past, our gender and instincts, and our right brain. She is the creature at whose whim we fall in love with totally inappropriate individuals or totally appropriate ones. This creature is pre-verbal; she only howls or moans, grumbles, or blissfully purrs. She is ancient; mine looks like a female Chewbacca from *Star Wars*. If she is happy, we have a lot of psychic and physical energy; if she is unhappy, we have barely enough energy to climb out of bed in the morning. If she is not in the mood to go on living, we can die without even getting sick first. So of course one must find out what it is that she needs to thrive.

This all-powerful entity is bored to death with our modern jobs. She sleeps throughout the day on her bed, unruly, woolly, and needy. She demands attention, so we give her coffee and doughnuts and sweets of all kinds, which work on her for a while, but not for long. She wants to be touched, made love to, entertained, and instructed. By the time we get home from work, she is on the warpath. She is hungry, tired, mad, and withdrawing. We resign ourselves dutifully to start dinner and take care of the kids (well, she comes out for kids, as well as pets).

The best thing to do for her is to take a brisk walk after work. She comes out of her stupor for Nature. She likes eveningtime outdoors best. She likes the moon and the stars, company, and good food. She likes shopping, because it reminds her of ancient foraging.

Wild Woman is not a workhorse. She is not even civilized. She is all the genes from the far-away ancestors her immortal body knows. She carries in her body memories of your grandmother's walk or her auburn hair, or your mother's entrancing eyes. She remembers the skinny feet of your great-grandfather on your father's side. You need her to go on with vigor for you to have enough energy to live, laugh, and love well. You and she are the most recent sprout of your ancestors on the Tree of Life, the last little green leaf on the edge of the bough. However, there is also a trunk, as well as all the other branches and leaves on the Tree. Those represent our ancestors. We are all part of the same life force. The Wild Woman controls everything important, from healing to ecstasy.

The Wild Woman loves a ritual, the chanting and the humming, the shared breath. She loves dancing on bare earth, large and small bonfires, and billowing incense climbing to the sky. She wakes up for play, shopping, physicality, fun, and love. It is difficult to go to work with a creature like that controlling you.

We all do it—but it's not easy.

We need to get closer to this mighty ancient creature and make her our friend. We need to discover how we can incorporate her into our daily lives and gain more confidence, have more energy, and gain access to our psychic powers.

The Wild Woman lives inside us all, but many of us were raised to be self-sacrificing women who find it hard to do things "just for ourselves." If you work with your Wild Woman, she will become your ally, a source of instinctive wisdom and energy. Every woman's Wild Woman is unique.

When you enter your workplace, your Wild Woman has a hard time adjusting. She is thrown from her warm bed into a steel building, where her blood's electricity is immediately disoriented.

3

The natural air she breathes is replaced by the air conditioning or heating system, her eyes no longer see enough relaxing greenery, the telephone's incessant ringing jars her nervous system, and the impersonal behavior of others alienates her. Then, to top it all, she has to do work-related tasks that have nothing to do with the great outdoors.

What would a Wild Woman appreciate in your office? What can you do to make her feel more grounded?

When you enter your office, take five minutes to establish your Wild Woman in your work area. Create a place where you put your special belongings or pictures. Wild Woman likes to watch over your things. Make a little nest of tiny, almost invisible things that are precious to you. One woman actually uses a real nest that she bought in a gift shop and that she filled with tiny semiprecious stones. She places her earrings there, too, because while she is working they interfere with her use of the telephone. Your special place can be just a spot on your desk or hidden on your bookshelves. Such an arrangement is not likely to attract the attention of your coworkers because it's small and unobtrusive. This is certainly better than having somebody ask you about the miniature Stonehenge you have built on your windowsill, leaving you in your three-piece power suit muttering under your breath about your "Wild Woman" needing attention!

This power spot can be a picture on your wall—something with woods or waterfalls, a picture of a mother holding a child, madonnas, rocks, the moon, or even food. Your Wild

Woman would love these images. Imagine her curled up inside this nesting, grounding place, and take a deep breath three times to signify that it is done. It is important to always make a green environment in your space, however small. Green plants are the best grounding.

Daily Maintenance of Wild Woman

While everybody else is going to get coffee, try instead a cup of jasmine tea. This tea is famous throughout the world as an antidepressant and aphrodisiac. It has caffeine but none of the acids coffee contains. Make a weak cup, though, because it is actually stronger than coffee.

Better still, avoid caffeine entirely and learn to manage your energy from within, listening to your body and feeling its fluctuations. Since you will probably still want something to drink, you should try other teas. The mints—peppermint or any of the others—can help wake you up in the morning. A cup of chamomile tea is useful if you are premenstrual or need calming down, and raspberry leaf tea will build up your female organs. Teas with fruit flavoring can liven up a dull afternoon. These days a wide variety of teas are available in supermarkets. Get a sampler box and try them.

As you go through your day, make sure there are some snacks available for your Wild Woman—things like almonds, raisins, dates, apples, figs, and so on. Do not go hungry. When you don't eat, it angers the Wild Woman, and she will be more demanding at the next mealtime. She has a way of overeating if she fears that you will be negligent about feeding her. She then tries to eat ahead to make up in advance for the missed foods.

If you have sugar cravings, it is the Wild Woman who is needy. Keep a bottle of honey in your desk and take a small spoonful when you want to reach for those deadly pastries in the cafeteria. Take the honey on your tongue and mentally send a message to the Wild Woman, saying, "This is for you, beloved." Lick the spoon and enjoy it as slowly as you can. Honey kills sugar cravings instantly, and it is an excellent brain food.

The Wild Woman needs not only food and drink but also air.

During the day, if you get angry with somebody, or some work-related problem makes you lose your balance, take at least three good deep breaths and come back to your images of the nest, earth, or wilderness. Breathe all the way down to the base of your spine; let the energy flow into all parts of your body. If you can step outside, do it, even if it is just on a small balcony or just outside the workplace. Stepping outside will reconnect your entire system with life. Do not live only in your head.

Make a new commitment to go on walks and week-end hikes, to be in nature and move your body in space. Exercise in a way that is not regimented. Learn natural movements that are much more comforting for the Wild Woman. Make sure you get hugs and kisses. Wild Woman likes to smooch. It stimulates her. Sign up for festivals, register for workshops, and give Wild

Woman space in your spiritual life, too. Keep her image and her needs in your mind.

In the following chapters we will refer to Wild Woman again and again. Her powers, her deeds, and her spells shall be known.

Monday

★　★　★　★　★　★　★　★　★　★　★

Feeling Grounded

Monday's Energy: Grounding Yourself

It's Monday, the first day of the week, the very one that you know the Fates should have delayed a few days longer so that you could live more during the weekend. Your co-workers arrive with bleary eyes and frowning. Everybody is guzzling coffee like liquid manna. You are right in thinking it's unjust the way your life has to be sacrificed for a "job," leaving you hardly time for anything else. Just when you start feeling like yourself again, boom, the weekend is over, and Monday is calling you back into the rat race.

Mondays are not meant to be focused on projects and left-brain activities like your job. The day was named after the moon: it's Moonsday, and as such it is a dreamy, introspective kind of time. You are naturally thinking about what you did over the weekend. Friends and family will have left you with many preoccupations, so it should be no surprise when thoughts that have nothing to do with the office come to mind.

Monday's Meaning: What to Do with Monday Energy or Lack Thereof

Monday is literally "Moonsday." The moon governs emotions, wildlife, fertility, and the life-giving waters. It's a good time for emotional processing, a good time to conduct meetings, both social and professional, or support groups. Slowly ease back into the workplace by catching up on correspondence and follow-ups and by nurturing old projects that are already under way.

The moon is our primary celestial sister. She reminds us of our body and our cycles, both physical and emotional. She governs the tides that move within us—our menstrual blood, our fertility, and our feelings. Incorporate a visit to a masseuse or a workout at the gym into your schedule. Make it an "honor thy body day." After work, celebrate the end of Monday with a self-nurturing bath.

Monday's Goddesses

The Goddess of the moon is *Diana*, the lovely huntress of the night: she who runs ahead of the winds, she who is hunting for high goals, she whose arrows never fail. "Dia" means holy, and "Anna" means mother; Diana is the original eternal virgin mother. Diana (her name in the Roman Empire and medieval Europe), or Artemis (her name in Greek), was originally a forest goddess. Her sacred animals are the countless creatures of the woods, especially the deer, bear, and hare. Talk to her on Monday by lighting a white candle, and she will give you strength.

You have heard about the goddess of the earth, deep-breasted *Gaia*, she of prophecy and foresight. She is considered to be the oldest of all goddesses; in fact, she is the living planet on which we are living. This concept of a living interconnected earthy divine being, our starship mother, is shared by all ethnic groups around the world. The Earth Goddess bears many names and has many stories. Call on her to help you feel grounded in your personal strength.

Monday's Scent

Your Wild Woman has a well-developed sense of smell. One way to prepare for the stresses and anxieties of the working day is to use carefully chosen scents. These scents will act as your personal shield against crowded rooms or invasion of your private workspace. The scent of your essence is very important; be sure not to get a synthetic chemical imitation, which will only give you headache. Order your scents from specialized shops. Doing this is more trouble and costs a little extra, but the scents will last you a long time, and your Wild Woman can tell the difference.

When you wear a scent, don't just dab it on; make a wish. Bless your ears for understanding by putting a little essence on them, bless your forehead so you will keep thinking clearly, and bless your legs by putting a little oil

behind your knees so that you may walk safely with a spring in your step.

For Monday, the scent of jasmine flowers can help lift the spirit into a joyous state, full of expectant energy. Begin the work week with jasmine. The essence of jasmine flowers can be used against fear and paranoia, pessimism, low self-confidence, and emotional suffering.

Of course, on Monday we don't want a nation full of office workers all smelling of a single scent. So if you are more drawn to roses or carnations, of course you should use them. The scents I am mentioning are only suggestions. Scents are personal; you must wear what makes you feel the best. For each day, choose whatever scent turns you on.

Bach Flower Remedies, by Dr. Edward Bach, offers many solutions for psychic problems that involve using different flower essences to heal the emotional body. Dr. Bach believed that illness happens because of conflict between the soul and the mind. He saw the remedies as a spiritual and mental effort. The Bach remedy for Monday is a few drops of Larch or Water Violet to boost self-confidence.

Monday's Gems

Mother Earth has created gems that have a calming effect on us. They include amethyst, hematite, tourmaline, quartz, red jasper, red or brown agate, amber, malachite, and jade. These are all semiprecious stones that you can pick up very reasonably at rock shops, gift shops, or mineral shows. Collect samples of these gems for your office; hold them in your hand, place them in your grounding place, and put them all around you.

Everyone can remember the kind of Monday at the office when the stress level is so high that you feel you will spit sparks if someone rubs you the wrong way. You can't focus or concentrate; everything that happens disturbs or distracts you. You feel spacy, nervous, or confused. Whether because of a project that wasn't completed on Friday or a huge proposal due at the end of the week, you need to get "grounded" again, or you won't get any work done.

With the Monday gem, *hematite,* the cure is very simple. Find a moment when you can sit at your desk without being disturbed. Kick off your shoes. Sit in a relaxed, balanced position with your eyes closed. Take a piece of hematite in each hand, and for a moment all you have to do is sit, observing your breathing. Breathe in to a steady count of four, hold it for two beats, then let it out for four beats and hold once more. Repeat this until you can feel yourself centered in your body.

Monday's Color

Color has a great deal to do with how we feel. Feelings are influenced not only by what colors we are looking at but also by what we are wearing. When you want to influence the feelings of others, the colors you choose that morning are important, for they will have a physical impact on everyone who sees you. A color chosen for a particular purpose doesn't have to constitute your entire outfit—a bold scarf will invoke feelings as well.

Blue green (teal) says, "Step aside, I am here, and I can handle everything." Wearing it promotes trust. It makes people believe in you. It stimulates your own practicality and helps you to maintain your spiritual practices.

Turquoise (bright greenish blue) is the color with the highest feminine vibration, the creative principle proudly stimulated. This color makes you an eternal student of life, calms you down, and reduces stress. Turquoise is good for workaholics, because it helps one to keep work in perspective; it increases analytical insight and even logic! How is that for the highest feminine qualities?

Royal blue is much like dark blue in its effects, but bolder. It is a color that suggests authority coupled with generosity, a color for a queen. Wearing royal blue, you are perceived as energetic and powerful but not forbidding. It helps you to clarify your thinking and deal with organization and structure. It is a good color for an administrator, not quite so overpowering as purple.

Light or sky blue is an ethereal shade that can temper the effect of the other blues. It suggests delicacy, clarity, and precision and raises the atmosphere to a more spiritual level. Wear it when you need to feel bright and youthful but remain fully in charge. It will make people want to be helpful without encouraging them to take liberties.

Peach is a stabilizing color. It is seen as calming and affluent; banks love to use it. It communicates that all is well. Peach is reassuring and safe. In peach you come across as trustworthy and prosperous.

Why Monday Is a Day for Grounding Yourself

The root of all of our existence is the part of our bodies that is most concerned with making use of the food we eat and eliminating what is left over. It is the seat of attachment for our energy bodies and, by extension, the key to our physical survival, prosperity, and excellence. This area is the beginning of our power system. I am speaking of the butt! It has often been devalued by metaphysicians, who look down on it as the "lowest" of powers from which one can operate. The reason for this prejudice is because the root chakra is located at the base of our spines—the part that supports us as we sit in our office chairs! The first lesson is not to ignore your power base. In our sacred bodies, no parts are inferior. The art of living involves working in the world, honoring our bodies, nourishing ourselves with food, friendship, and love.

Now increase your body awareness—especially your consciousness of your first power center, the place where your body is supporting your weight, the point of contact between you and the chair. Focus your consciousness on that area and then, very slowly, let it drop downward like a root. You are heading for Mother Earth, and even if you are sitting on the twenty-seventh floor, your mind can send your awareness down through all those floors to bedrock. Let your consciousness sink into the soil. Feel yourself putting a root into the earth. Feel her dark strength cradling you. Then begin to draw energy up through that root.

When you have enough energy, draw that extension of your awareness back up into your body again. You will find that you feel rested, and it is now much easier to remember who you are and focus on the task at hand.

Monday's Spells for Survival

1. Blessing on a Project Proposal

Since Monday is a day of beginnings, this seems a good time to introduce a spell for getting your work going as well. A bona fide office witch, Laurel, gave me the following spell: Take the proposal in its final form and start drawing an invisible pentagram on it with your finger. The pentagram has been demonized by Hollywood and the born-again Christians. Its original meaning, however, is the balance of the elements and the spirit in our lives.

First, draw an arrow upward from the lower-left corner to the top, then down to the lower-right corner, then up to the far left and across to the right and down to complete the star.

In this drawing, you are using the rune Tiwaz ↑ the sacred warrior energy, to make the pentagram of magic. The spiritual warrior knows the right way, the proper way. You acknowledge that the universe always makes the first move, but you add your own. Tiwaz is the rune of justice and dedication. The old Vikings used to paint it on their spears before battle. However, because this *is* a rune of justice, before you invoke it you should be very sure that your proposal is a fair one.

Next you circle the pentagram, because the circle is the blessing of completion. Finally, you put on the top another smaller circle with the equal-armed cross in it, which is the symbol of the earth and money. Runes can be extremely useful in doing office magic and have the advantage of looking ornamental.

2. A Ritual of Eating

In ancient times people offered the gods portions of their food by burning it. Eating was a form of prayer. Today we ignore our food. While we are eating, we read the newspaper or visit with friends. Every so often, use your lunch break just to eat. Sit down with your lunch and bless it by saying something like this: "May this food I am about to eat support me in health, wealth, and wisdom, the divine three. Blessed be." Actually, what I say is a little less poetic: "Thank you, tuna fish, for dying for me; thank you, onions, for dying for me; thank you, wheat, for dying for me," and so on. Say these words silently—you don't have to let everyone know what you are doing by praying loudly in the cafeteria.

Now, visualize your Wild Woman coming out of her hiding place, picking up the food, and eating it slowly. In spite of my strict upbringing, I always make satisfied sounds when I eat, like "hmmmmm" or "yum yum." My aunt Titi used to pay me money to eat in a civilized way—you know, using forks and knives and not making noise while I eat. But now that I am grown up, I have returned to the way I appreciated my food when I was a young girl. My Wild Woman must eat; she must come out and have her food. "Hmmmm," I hum when a bite tastes good.

17

The Wild Woman needs her food pleasures, and if she feels you are depriving her she will get even and add some more flesh on you just in case you have that zany idea about starving her again. Avoid obvious fatty foods, dead foods, and pastries, but please don't go on any diets. Women are supposed to be all different shapes and sizes, round or tall, fleshy or small. Read *The Beauty Myth* by Naomi Wolf and reject our culture's oppressive ideals of beauty.

Drink a hearty glass of water after you have eaten. I recommend a cup of raspberry tea in the afternoon. It builds up your female organs and influences your moods for the better.

3. The Dance of Life

When your work is done, do not prolong it beyond what is required of you. Go home and take a shower to signify to your Wild Woman that she can come out now. Don't turn on your TV; it will help you relax, but it will also slow down your metabolism so that you won't have the will to get up and move. Take a walk, get physical. Encourage your friends to join you in nonalcoholic activities, such as walks, dinners, or going out to the movies. Your Wild Woman appreciates exercise because your body is her body, but don't make doing your exercises into a second job and feel guilty when you don't feel like doing them.

My friend Bella told me she had no energy at the end of the day. She would go home and collapse. I told her to make an agreement with herself, to say, "Okay, I don't feel like it, but for an hour after I get off work I'm going to go to a place where they have dancing and hang out." When you feel other

Wild Women and Wild Men dancing around you, it will help energize you.

If you live alone, it's a good idea to have a cat or a dog. A cat is better if you don't have time to take walks with your animal; you have to get out and walk the dog no matter what. Animals bring out the Wild Woman. They connect you to the Goddess's other creations, the animal world; they soothe you and comfort you with their direct body contact. They remind you of what's important in life—food, love, health, and companionship.

4. Spell for Your Moon Days

There you are in your civilized office; all around you is paperwork, and the phones are ringing. Just when you want to forget about your body and enter the mind's realm, you feel the unmistakable primal ooze between your legs. You have just received your moon blood!

Your Wild Woman is out in force. One woman, Margaret, hung a calendar on the wall of her office and noted the days of her period with big red letters. This made the statement "Yes, I have moon times" in a powerful, self-respecting way. If you hide things, they seem less normal. If you allow them to be in the open, they become more accepted. It *does* take a lot of nerve.

Another friend, Lilian, complained to me that each time she voiced a strong opinion, a co-worker would accuse her of being "on the rag." To have any unwanted discussion about your moon blood is sexual harassment. But when men hold your blood against you, they are expressing fear of your emotional/female/cyclical nature.

19

The days of your period are the best time to cast spells because this is when your Wild Woman is strongest. You are filled with emotional energy, which is the true fuel for magic. So for each period look up a spell to do to make your life easier.

To make your flow easier, drink herbal teas of yarrow, comfrey, chamomile, and the always wonderful red raspberry leaf tea. Health-food stores have many good herbal mixes for use during your moon bloods. Use them and be glad.

For example, when you begin your period, light a red candle and say:

This is the blood that gives life.
This is the blood that carries the memories of my ancestors.
This is the blood that will heal my soul.
This is the blood of the mother who gives all life.

Now take some raspberry tea and sip it, visualizing health and well-being spreading throughout your ovaries and womb. Take the candle into the bathroom and take a hot bath; pamper yourself in the candle's rosy light.

When you have relaxed for a while in the light of your candle, say:

This is the blood that connects me to my power.
This is the blood of the Goddess, who heals all wounds.
This is my blood, the blood of my wildness,
And I give birth to myself.

Every day that you bleed, celebrate with baths, words, hot teas, and sleep and dream on a scented pillow. Eat baked sweet potatoes, which will help balance your hormones. Feel your own importance and your connection to the moon and hence to the universe.

5. Relaxing

If you cannot rest at night, your body and spirit will soon be exhausted and you will get sick. When we sleep is when we visit with our dreams, which is almost more important than actual bed rest. Scientists who have studied sleep have found that people who were deprived of REM sleep, when dreams occur, suffered from fatigue and depression.

Construct a *dream pillow* for yourself. In an herb shop buy about a pound and a half of the herb *artemisia vulgaris* (*mugwort*). You can mix the mugwort with other herbs such as heliotrope, jasmine, cinquefoil, and the petals of marigolds and roses. Get out your favorite pillow, mix the herbs in with the down, and sew the pillow up again. If you sleep on this pillow every night, you will find that your dreams will be in full color and often healing and prophetic.

To help you sleep, drink a cup of chamomile tea with honey. It is a gentle nervine, a brew that is pleasantly comforting. If you are too wired for chamomile to work alone, mix catnip (which calms humans) and hops and drink a tea made of that. Sleeping tea mixes are available in health-food stores everywhere. Don't use sleeping pills. You cannot dream lucidly when you are drugged.

If you are a workaholic who cannot stop thinking about work even after you have gone home, if thoughts jitter in your brain like a cat on a hot tin roof, and you cannot unhook from your daily worries, take the Bach remedy of a few (eight to ten) drops of *vervain*. It is said that essence of vervain puts things into perspective, brings back playfulness, and puts restraints on what is unchecked. It is a great remedy if you are an obsessive person.

Now your Wild Woman can survive your boring modern schedule and not feel abused. She is not going to be plotting how to trip you up by sabotaging your meetings with fatigue, overwhelming you with hunger, or making you burst out with something embarrassing in public to vent anger. As a daily reward, let her take a lot of time in the bathroom, or frequent spas. Use scented waters to wash your body and sea salt in your bath for your muscles, or Epsom salts and baking soda if you worked out and need special relaxation.

As the last act of your Monday, light a white or pink candle in front of your Goddess image, which may be a single rose or some other flower that reminds you of Mother Nature, and say:

> Dearest Goddess, I close my eyes, but yours are open
> to watch over me while I am asleep. Thank you for
> my life and the blessings you have sent me, and
> thank you for the blessings yet to come.

With this tuck yourself in, let a cat curl up next to you or, if you have a partner, kiss her or him goodnight. And sleep.

6. Spell for Grounding Yourself with Gaia

Gaia is the All Creator. She created herself out of chaos, then she created heaven and called him Uranus, and then she took him for her lover and thus conceived all the gods of heaven.

She created the sea and, naming him Pontus, took him for her lover; thus she created the deities of the ocean. Homer wrote:

> I shall sing of Gaia, Universal Mother, firmly
> founded,
> Oldest of all the holy Ones.

I think Gaia is the perfect Goddess to work with for office survival. In order to venerate Gaia, you must put your bare feet on dirt at least once a week. Even just standing barefoot on the brown dirt in the parking lot is better than no contact at all. When you do this, remember that no matter how undervalued she is today, Gaia's power still rules, and her natural laws still govern.

At home or at the office Gaia can have her special mini-shrine, built with a stone or two, feathers fallen from birds to represent the heaven, and a shell or pearl to represent the sea. You can enter this small universe with your weary soul and pray to Gaia when you are in trouble. Here you may keep your special aroma bottle and the bottle of your favorite Bach flower remedy, all the tools you need for your wellness at work. Here you can rest and ground in the middle of a workday.

You need not perform big rituals for Gaia. She is more likely to take delight if you appreciatively peel an orange and eat every bite with gratitude to the source of this food, Gaia.

You can make the paper you use on the job a symbol of Gaia, because paper is made from her trees. Write her name on a white piece of paper with your wish and place it under her stones. Keep it there until the wishes come true.

If you are having trouble, write the name of the problem on a piece of paper backwards nine times, then find a lone spot in nature and bury the paper deep in Gaia's body. She has a way of grounding troubles as well. In return, pick up other people's garbage in the parks as a service to Gaia. Recycle everything possible as a religious rite. For your efforts, Gaia will reward you with robust vitality and longevity.

Lean against trees with your spine against the trunk and imagine your energy merging with that of the tree. Feel your energy climbing inside the tree and reaching to the tip of the treetop. Then look out and revel in this feeling. Trees are the lungs of the Goddess, and you can breathe with her. Increased energy and higher vitality are your rewards for such adventures.

A Meditation to Discover and Define Your Wild Woman

To discover your Wild Woman, lie down on your back somewhere comfortable and safe and take a deep breath that reaches all the way into your toes. Wiggle your toes and relax them. Take another deep breath into your legs, all the way up to your thighs, and relax them, too. Now, take a breath into your thighs and hips and relax them; take another into your chest and heart and relax them. Take another breath into your arms and shoulders and relax them. Now take a breath that fills your neck and relax your neck. Finally, breathe deeply into your face and brain; relax your brain, scalp, and face. Now imagine that you are smoke and, like a curl of a smoke cloud, slip out of your body through the top of your head and rise, rise, rise.

You have risen above your own body, and you can see yourself lying there. You now rise over your own house. Now you are looking down from a bird's-eye view at the familiar features of your neighborhood: the treetops and the tops of the houses below.

Whooooshh . . . like a streak of light now you find yourself in a deep forest, with birds happily singing, a waterfall nearby, caves and caverns, and old hollow tree trunks. Here in this safe place you abide in peace. I have given you a magic basket that holds all you will need. Feel the peace. Now feel that there is another being there with you. Somebody female . . . Look for her there, feel for her, search for her, find her. Perhaps this creature is in some opening? A tree trunk? A cave? Or by a waterfall? Look around in your own way and find an opening where you feel this female presence is living.

When you sense where she is hiding, enter the opening gently and nonthreateningly. In your magic basket I have placed all kinds of presents, so now you can reach in and trust your hand to find an appropriate gift for this creature. Approach her in the dark, and she will reveal her form to you soon enough. When she does, introduce yourself and hold out a present. Wild Woman is nonverbal, but she understands presents very well.

Wild Woman's appearance may surprise you. Take a good look. She may be young or old, a wild animal or a magical animal. As you visit her, she may appear in many different forms.

Now I want you to observe how Wild Woman receives her gift from you. What was it? Grapes? Melons? Chocolate? Or red pantyhose? Endless significant and humorous gifts have been given to Wild Woman throughout the years. Remember to note your own.

At this point you should tell Wild Woman that you will return often to see her. Make a solemn promise. She may mock you for your sudden devotion, but she will accept it. Then take her hand and lead her outside of the enclosure, into the light part of the forest.

Here Wild Woman and you can perform a sacred dance. Dance with your Wild Woman, any way you can imagine. Jump up treetops and down, slide across the lakes, fly up in the air, mirror each other, or just dance together. Make a show of it. Now calm down. Rest awhile. However, before you go, you should ask Wild Woman for a magical talisman. What did she give?

Now it is your turn to give Wild Woman a protection talisman that she can wear around her neck. Wild Woman spooks easily. She may get scared if people disapprove of her and give her the evil eye. So you should reward her with a little red flannel bag with some magical stones inside (if you don't have a real bag, you can use an imaginary one). Choose your favorite gems, a bird feather, or some other natural object. This will help Wild Woman repel attacks on her while you work. The exchange of such magical presents cements your bond.

"How can I come back to you most easily?" you ask. The answer comes, and now it's clear how you will return. Say goodbye. You rise like smoke and, hushhhhhh, you are back where you began. Slipping back in through the head with a deep breath, entering the face, the brain, the neck, the shoulders, the stomach, the chest, the hips, and the legs and thighs and toes. Wiggle your toes. Now you are back home.

Breathe deeply in and out. Breath connects you to life.

Open your eyes and move about. How does your body feel? Can you hold up your physical body with your psychic one? Write down what went on in your mind and share it with somebody. Think about it again. Go back to see what has changed. Is Wild Woman the ancient friend who heals all wounds? Or is she dependent on you for your handling and caring?

This first visit is the beginning of a series of explorations from which you'll form a more conscious connection to the ancient self, the old one, the eternal one, the only one. Developing a continuous relationship with one's Wild Woman is a skill, but one no harder than taking care of your cat. Our dear self-esteem must draw her mighty breath from this deep well; the wilderness in women must be reclaimed.

Tuesday

* ★ ★ ★ ★ ★ ★ ★ ★ ★ ★ ★

Work and Will

Tuesday's Energy: Will, Ego, Humor

Have you ever noticed that the work week really begins on Tuesday? You have lingered over Monday's emotions long enough—recovered from the weekend and grounded yourself. Now it's time to get some work done. Set your goals. Make an accounting of your abilities and opportunities. Apply your will to your situation. Make a move. Assert your power and effectiveness. I recommend that you clean your apartment or house after work on Tuesday.

On Tuesday we enter the rat race, fight our own battles, attack piles of work, give orders, make our wills known. We go after the things we want and cast spells to attract the things we need.

In your solar plexus you feel power, or you may sense the gnawing lack of control over your own destiny. Here is the source of ambition and competition. This is the seat of your own will.

29
.

Beware of talk against the ego. If you didn't need to have a powerful will, Mother Nature would not have bothered to develop one in you. You cannot make a living in the world without an ego. It takes an ego to say yes or no.

Humor lives in the solar plexus. Remember the kind of laughter that rocked you so deeply it made you fall down and laugh even harder? That laughter rocked you from your solar plexus. Anxiety makes its presence felt there, too. It is the place where you experience butterflies before an important meeting or job interview.

Tuesday Means Justice

The second day of the work week was named after the northern god Tyr. He is the spirit of justice. Tyr's nature is discipline and integrity—he is a peacekeeper and a spiritual warrior.

The Romans assigned the planet Mars to Tuesday. Mars governs courage, aggression, confrontation, the sex drive, activation, boldness, weapons, and military leadership as well as these professions: chemists and engineers, police, construction workers, butchers, dentists, and iron and steel workers. Clearly, Tuesday is a day on which a lot can get done!

Exercise justice by remembering that women must learn to support each other and play like teammates without destroying each other's achievements. The opening of doors for the next generation by the old-boy network is what has given men the power in the business world. Having more women in more powerful positions improves the status of all women.

Oya, a Wild Woman in the Marketplace, a Powerful Goddess for Tuesday

Among the Yoruba people of Africa, where most of the trade was traditionally conducted by women, the Goddess of the marketplace is Oya. Oya is a lady of many talents—she assists the leader of the market women in negotiating with the authorities and protects women in leadership positions. She can be pungent, persuasive, or downright violent when she appears as the Tornado Goddess, the lady of wind and fire. She is a Goddess of changes and transformations. Learn to balance her energies, and she will help you. Deny her, and she can wreck your business life.

Oya was married first to Ogun, the forge god. She pulled at the bellows as he hammered out tools. One day the war god, Shango, came along, and she liked him so well she left with him. Shango is a fire god, and Oya stole his lightning. She is also the Goddess of the Niger River. Sometimes she is the wise and courageous water buffalo who leads the herd, gentle when undisturbed but terrifying in her wrath.

Oya came to the New World with the Yoruba slaves and for safety's sake was identified with Our Lady of Candelaria, Saint Barbara, or Joan of Arc in the evolving religions of Santeria and Macumba, where she is called Iansa. She sometimes wears men's clothing, and she defends those who invoke her. She carries the spirits of the dead to their destination and can face down demons.

Oya's colors are the orange shades and burnt reds and purples. Her sacred number is nine. Invoke her for protection and energy when you need help to make an important deal or to win justice. When your life gets chaotic, make an altar to her with a purple candle and offer her some fresh fruit to calm things down. In a traditional Yoruba song she sings:

> Should anyone act with malice toward you,
> Just let me know;
> Should you want anything—
> Money, mates, children—
> Just call on me; call, "Oya, Oya."

> *(As sung by Awotunde Aworinde, translated
> by Judith Gleason, in* Oya: In Praise of an
> African Goddess.)

If you need Oya's help, call her name: "Oya, Oya—Heyi Eepa! What a Goddess!"

★ ★ *Tuesday's Scent*

Honeysuckle is sacred to Jupiter (Juno), the planet of expansion, wealth, communication, and power. It combines well with Tuesday's Mars energy. Honeysuckle is a very feminine power scent. This scent feeds Wild Woman with messages of fulfillment so she wants to eat less, so this scent stimulates weight loss. When folk magic talks about the sweet smell of money, it is talking about the sweet honeysuckle. In the office this scent will establish around you an atmosphere of wealth, well-being, psychic awareness, and prosperity. All you have to do is wear it or inhale it and visualize money, visualize more power for yourself, the gentle leadership that flows effortlessly, the kind others are honored to follow. It is grounding yet uplifting; the scent is wild enough and yet tame enough. But remember, a little goes a long way.

To repel sexual advances, wear *lavender*. I know it is the scent of trust, but it is also the antidote for lust. When men are around lavender, they start thinking of their mothers and are turned off. In North Africa women use this scent to guard against mistreatment from their husbands. The wearer and those around her are stimulated in the direction of health, love, celibacy, peace, and heightening the conscious mind.

Tuesday's Gem

There are many other semiprecious and precious stones that can really help out in the office. We all know about worry beads, pet rocks, worry balls, and the like. However, the most socially acceptable and visually beautiful art from earth that you can display is the *clear quartz crystal*. This is the mother of all healings. Its vibrations affect the seen and unseen worlds; it will influence you positively in whatever is needed to balance, to empower, to build confidence.

Keep a clear quartz crystal on your table, in a corner, or even on the floor behind your chair where nobody sees it. This crystal can be your powerhouse, your special secret place, your psychic oasis in the concrete jungle. Rub your hands on it; hold it; absorb its power. Visualize this earth jewel infusing you with healing, relaxation, excitement, effectiveness, and good fortune. Use it as a wish stone. Before a consultation or a proposal, hold it in your hands and breathe deeply in and out, opening your mind to its effects.

Say this three times:

Clear stone, clear light,
Let my purpose be strong and bright.
Let my mind be focused, my soul satisfied.

Tuesday's Color

If your purpose is to stand out in the crowd, to be in the public eye and express your personal power, or to restore your physical stamina, wear *red*—any and all reds. This color will say, "Look at this woman. She is daring; she is magnificent, strong, and desirable." However, like any really powerful statement, red sometimes works better in moderation. In most business situations, a completely red outfit would seem too flashy, but a red blouse or scarf is an accent that will brighten up everyone's day. If you want to protect yourself from draining persons, ward off outside stress, and stimulate sensuality, wear *maroon*.

Black is the color of authority, mystery, and the clergy. When you wear black, you are saying to the world that your opinions are definitive: you are wise, trustworthy, and spiritual. You rely not on your outside beauty but on your inner strengths. Black can be a very good color if you are in authority and need to stay that way.

Let's say you want to *protect* your emotions, to repel personal and sexual comments. You don't want people to come up and feel free to interfere in your life; rather, you want to inspire respect and create a certain distance. In this case, wear *dark blue*. Guess why the police wear that color? You can find lovely feminine dark blues. This color prevents fatigue on the job and helps you keep focused and relaxed. When you wear dark blue, you will feel more authoritative, your wisdom will flow, and you will be more aware of yourself.

Tuesday's Spells for Will and Justice

1. Purifying the Office

The office is full of trouble—the computers are often down; your co-workers are talking behind your back; your boss doesn't seem to hear you. People walk past you as if you weren't there, and your projects don't get the cooperation they need. What's wrong? Is the entire world set against you?

Here is a perfect opportunity for you to apply your willpower to set things right. All the world is made up of energy. The form things take depends on their vibrational frequency. We are going to set up some harmonizing and purifying vibrations in your workspace.

At home, take a small dish of spring water, which you can buy in grocery stores, and soak in it a sprig of lemon verbena or some dried lemon verbena herb. If you can't get herbs, put a pinch of sea salt (or even table salt) in the water.

Lemon verbena is an herb that breaks up evil vibrations and negativity. Salt from the sea is also a physical and magical purifier, as is seawater itself, which is all the more powerful because it is living water. Hold your hand over the water and say something like this:

> Water wash clean! Wash away the discord from my office. Let everyone who quarreled now make up. Let everything that hasn't been working now start up again. (Add to this prayer whatever is particularly wrong with your office.) In the name of Diana, so mote it be.

Come to work early before anybody else is there and scatter this blessed water around the office by dipping a sprig of any green (pine for example) or any flower (marigold) into it to use as a sprinkler. Wear sandalwood oil as your perfume and burn a little sandalwood or sage incense. Let the smoke percolate through the space and purify it from the unseen vibrations left by troublemakers.

Leave and enter again when others will witness your arrival, so no suspicion can fall on you. If anybody mentions the "strange" smell in the office, just smile and say nothing. The troubles will evaporate with the water and dissipate with the smoke.

An alternative office purifier is a cup of piping hot peppermint tea with some lemon in it. If you have to purify the place without letting on what you are doing, walk nonchalantly around the office, letting the mist from your cup act as your incense, and send your thoughts of purification up with the mist. Use the same prayer as above, but silently.

2. Protecting Your Belongings

A spell to protect the things you keep in the office may sometimes be necessary. Things can get misplaced or even stolen. To prevent your drawers and files from being disturbed, wait until the new or waxing moon. Purchase an herb called "dragon's blood reed" at an occult supply store. This is the reddish, sweet-smelling resin from the fruit of the dragon tree found in the Canary Islands and Indonesia. Sometimes it comes rolled up in exotic leaves, looking really primal. Break off little pieces of it and hide them in the bottoms of your drawers, shelves, and files. Put your hands (the conductors of your will) over the drawers and say:

> Dragon's blood, watch and ward
> As the dragon guards her hoard.
> Touch not what belongs to me,
> As I will, so mote it be!

3. Recovering Stolen Goods

If you have just discovered that something has been stolen from you, light a black candle at home and write on it, "The one who took my (missing object)," and burn a third of the candle for three nights in a row. As you watch the candle burn, say:

37

There is nowhere to hide.
There is nowhere to go.
Return my (name of the stolen object)
Or all will know!

Finish burning the candle, then gather some of its wax drippings. Take them to work and place them unobtrusively where you think the person may have taken your property and will be likely to step on them. If it is something intangible, such as an opportunity, that was stolen from you, reword the spell and say, "Don't take what is mine."

4. Protecting Your Job

It happens. The boss wants to get you; the company needs to downscale; you look vulnerable. As soon as you get wind of the danger, light a small blue candle on your desk. Draw on your blue candle the rune of Elhaz ᛉ . This is the rune of protection. Remain aware that timely action and correct conduct are the true protections for the spiritual warrior. Start wearing blue to work. Think blue; visualize a blue mist around yourself.

Then get even more sneaky. Bake or buy "love" muffins flavored with lemon or lime. What will make them love muffins is the spell you are going to put on them. You may want to do this at home, where you have privacy.

Light a blue candle. Place the muffins on the same table, hold your hands over them, and breathe three times deeply, calling up your Wild Woman from the depths of your psyche. Then say:

I call upon my ancestors, grandmothers and
    grandfathers;

> I call my loved ones, both dead and alive,
> To enter my life and avert the danger, avert the evil
>   eye.
> Let my livelihood be safe and let me be satisfied.
> All who partake of these muffins will help me to keep
>   my job.

Repeat this three times while you sprinkle the muffins with lemony sugar or powdered lime, both traditionally believed to turn the heart toward love. Feel your will flowing through your hands into the baked goods. Any baked goods with a spell on them will work. How about baking cookies and drawing on each of them the rune of Elhaz, the rune of protection? Your co-workers will think it's just a fancy pastry design.

Distribute these muffins to your friends and enemies at the coffee station. Visualize these people adoring you. Visualize your boss changing her or his mind about letting you go. Keep wearing blue. However, never tell what you have done, or you will cancel the spell.

5. Fighting Sexual Harassment

Sexual harassment spells are not for women who don't want to fight back. In the spells against sexual harassment, we will be using natural materials such as our own urine; because it contains your DNA, because it stands for elimination; and because traditionally menstrual blood, urine, saliva, and sexual secretions were considered very potent tools in creating magic. If you have had enough and are ready to use woman magic to fight back, I shall withhold nothing

from you. If you can hold down a job on your own, you are old enough to hear what real witches can do.

Sexual harassment is a problem that has made a lot of news. Usually it is done to women by men, but sometimes by men to other men or by a woman to a man. I am going to use the generic term *he* here because the great majority of the criminal offenses are committed by males. The law offers one way to get justice, but the process can be lengthy and painful for all concerned. Perform all the spells I give you here at the waning and the dark moon. (Check with a moon calendar to determine when these take place.)

A. Phase One: Protecting Yourself from Sexual Harassment

If your boss or a co-worker is harassing you sexually or hurting you in some way, it is reasonable for you to wish this person would stop or go make a living elsewhere. In the past, the offended woman had to give up her job and move on. Feminist witches do not think that is right, so instead, you are going to send the harasser on a long journey and get him to change jobs or even professions, just so long as he is out of your life.

1. Hot Foot Spell   Purchase from an occult supply store or specialty catalogue something called *Hot Foot powder.* It is a white powder that will sink undetectably into the carpet, and the idea is to sprinkle it someplace where your harasser will walk. Before you sprinkle the powder, hold your hands over it, project your will into the substance, and say three times:

You will now rise, you will now walk,
You will now fly, you will now disappear.
Out of my life, out of this office,
Out of this project, out of my world.
Blessed be!

If you know a place where this person would be happier, get a map of it and place a black candle over the spot. Write the harasser's name on it backward three times with a rusty nail. Visualize him getting an invitation or a job offer and falling in love with the new place or becoming eager to be gone from your place of work.

2. Stopping Verbal Harassment (or Gossip Against You in the Office)

It is not always obvious when sexual harassment begins. Often a hurtful remark designed to lower a woman's self-esteem is disguised as a "joke."

A friend of mine reported that her boss would come to her workspace, step right up close to her chair, and lean over her with his crotch pressed against her desk. She would immediately get up, suggest they move to a more appropriate place to talk, and make him follow her. The same man would also comment on her weight. "You should go to a gym and work out," he would say. "You are soft inside and outside." Another woman reported that her boss would comment on what she was wearing every day and trash her taste in clothes.

Women are fed up with feeling harassed at work. Here are a few tips on how to work against it if you are fed up, too. The violence of your reaction is what gives the power to the spell, but channeling these emotions can itself be taxing. If you are going to use this energy, use it to get rid of your own pain. Let your hatred, frustration, or fear flow through you to power the spell, and then release it completely. If you find yourself depressed or still obsessing about your experiences after you have done the spell, do some of the purifying and healing magic described elsewhere in this book.

The following spell was given to me by Luisah Teish, a Yoruba priestess and author of *Jambalaya*. Attention: We will be using pig's tongue from the butcher shop. If that is too icky for you, go to the next section.

Go to a butcher shop and buy a small pig's tongue. Take a piece of white paper and write the name of the harasser on it backward nine times with black ink. Cut open the tongue and rub it with black pepper inside and out. Smear a little of your own urine on the paper and fold it away from you until it's small enough to fit into the tongue. Now stuff the paper into the pig's tongue, holding the image of your harasser's tongue in mind. Take a rusty nail and press it into the tongue until it pierces through the whole thing, paper and all.

Take the prepared tongue and a shovel to a wild place—a state park, a desert, or as far as you can get from your house within a reasonable time. Dig a hole and bury the tongue deep in the earth. This is the grounding element in the spell. When you have buried the tongue, pee on it (or take a little urine in a small bottle with you from home and sprinkle it over the spot), imagining eliminating the harassment for good. Then leave and don't look back. Within a moon the harasser should change his behavior or leave the office.

3. Protective Scents Wear *bergamot oil* if you can. It is powerful enough to protect against all evil. When you put on the oil, visualize a peaceful interaction with your would-be harassers. If they inquire what you are wearing, say it's called "Strike Back" perfume, the newest thing on the market. Keep lemons and oranges in a bowl in your office. Your Wild Woman will like it, and the magical effect of the scent of citrus is protection.

It is also important to protect yourself against self-blame. The Bach flower remedy for this is six to ten drops daily of pine.

If this soft approach has failed, and the harassment continues, move up to witch's spell for protection Phase Two.

B. Phase Two: Combating Sexual Harassment

If you have tried all your personal spells and protections and the harassment continues, it's time to combine real-world action with magical action. Start documenting the harassment and create a paper trail of protests. Audiotape or videotape it if you can. Get a friend in the office to take photographs. Send the harasser a letter of protest witnessed by a lawyer. Collect witnesses. Join a support group against sexual harassment.

Think about what would be the most efficient solution for your own good. Listen to your feelings but don't ignore reality. What will serve you best? Here are some options.

1. Hot Foot Spell: Second Time Around Get some more Hot Foot powder and buy a small bottle of protection oil, a small bottle of double-crossing oil, a black candle in the shape of a man (or a woman, if she is the one who is attacking you), and some Black Arts incense.

Even though you may be cringing in your three-piece suit, your Wild Woman will have a ball with all this apparently irrational activity. Relax. This is a job for her.

Go home and create for this work a little space in which you can build a black altar with black tablecloths and a black candle. Have some Black Arts incense ready in a burner. Note that in this case the color black does not mean evil or have a racial meaning. It is a color that absorbs all others and therefore gets rid of things. It is the color of the universe.

With a rusty nail etch backward three times the name of your harasser on the black image candle. This candle stands only for the harasser. Anoint the candle with your urine (for elimination) and roll it in Hot Foot powder.

When darkness descends upon the world and the waning moon lazily sails across the sky, take a purification bath with lemon in the bath water. When you have emerged all relaxed and refreshed, stand before your altar. Now you must reach inside to where the pain the harassment has caused you is festering. Feel the power of your pain rising through you and appeal to the goddess as *Nemesis*.

Nemesis is the female principle of the universe that hunts down wrongdoers, especially those who have abused their power. Since she represents absolute justice, be very sure that you are in the right before you attract her attention. If your motives are not pure or the situation is not really serious, you may find her chasing you. Visualize her as an angry woman in black draperies. Now imagine your tormentor cowering before her. See her chasing him away from the city and across the world, giving him no rest until he is out of your life. If a harasser is female, the same spell will work with a female image candle. Nemesis is an equal opportunity equalizer.

Now pick up the black image candle and say:

> Nemesis, Angry Mother, to you I pray.
> At work (name) is hurting me.

(Here summarize what has happened, using examples from the evidence you have collected.)

> I need your wrath to right this wrong.
> Let me survive and thrive at my best.
> Nemesis, Mother of Justice, come!
> Chase (name) out of my realm!

Now light the incense and pass the image candle through its smoke, visualizing and identifying the candle with the person. Say:

> This is (name).
> He will stop abusing me.
> He will stop hurting me.
> If he cannot change this time,
> He will be gone, gone from my sight.
> I shall stay where I am now.
> The loss is his, not mine!

Light the candle now and say:

> As this flame burns down the wax,
> So the power of (name) will lapse.
> As this flame burns low,

So his power over me go,
And all my pain will disappear.
As this candle dies out at last,
I shall be free from this unjust harm!

Burn the candle down a third each night for three nights in a row. When the candle is all consumed, take some of the wax remnants, mix them with Hot Foot powder, and throw them in the path of the harasser. It won't matter who else steps on it. The spell isn't for them. Only the harasser will get this whammy—Nemesis knows who it is intended for. You could deliver the spell by taking the mix into his office and burying it in a flowerpot there, or you could sprinkle it underneath his desk. You only need a little bit—there's no need to be obvious. In magic the link is everything, and less can be more.

Wait for a moon for results. You must stop thinking about it. A spell must be "cast away" before it can return fulfilled. Do not obsess, but do keep documenting what you can.

2. Full-Force Hexing If the harassment still hasn't stopped, at the dark of the moon, or when you bleed, escalate to the following witch's whammy.

On the reality level, please make the appropriate moves to confront this guy with the evidence and involve the appropriate authorities. Make formal complaints. Talk to a lawyer. On the magical level, this time we are going to make a doll out of black cloth and stuff it with stinging herbs such as nettle, datura, and rue. You really need your Wild Woman to come out for this one. This is a hex for strong spirits to perform.

The doll will represent the harasser. Give it eyes (stitch on beads) and hair (some of his, if possible) and make it look like him—symbolically, of course. Anoint the doll with that double-crossing oil you purchased and say:

> This is now (name) in all his dealings. All that is done to this doll will happen to (name). His friends will turn on him, his family will reject him, and all his co-workers will turn away from him.

For nine nights in a row you have to perform spells over this doll. Doing this takes patience, and this hexing should really be used only if all else has failed. While casting the spells, anoint yourself daily with protection oil.

Each night lay the doll on a black cloth and sprinkle him with a little bit of graveyard dust. This is a powder that you can get from an occult supply store, or you can go to a cemetery and take a handful of earth from somewhere where there is no grave (if you take it from a grave, you may take home a ghost and involve an unknown element in this hex).

Now tie the hands of the doll behind his back and bind his feet with black cord. Say over the doll:

> Thus do I bind thee.
> Thus do I curse thee.
> Stop your harassment
> Or take your punishment.
> I bind your hands that they may not touch me.
> I bind your feet that you may not come near me.
> I bind your mouth that you may not speak against
>   me.
> I bind your penis that you may not lust after me.

I bind your heart that you may not hate me.
I bind your whole body that you may be powerless to
    harm me!

Burn black candles on the altar to the left and to the right of the doll. As you name his body parts, stick pins with black heads into the doll. Wrap him again in black cloth when you are finished and hide him where nobody can find him. (I can just see your cat dragging this around for fun when you have some dinner guests over.)

Nine nights in a row is a long time, and you will find yourself wanting to fudge it. The hexing will interfere with your nightly routine or your favorite show on TV. Do these spells before you settle down to relax. You may want to stop by the fifth night or the seventh. However, if your life is on the line, or at least your career, you have to stand up against the oppressors. The Wild Woman works best by repetition. She is happy and proud to defend you.

When the nine nights are finally done and the black candles have burned down to the quick, gather a little wax from them and take your doll on a long ride far, far away, preferably out of town. Dig a hole where nobody can find it or find a cemetery and dig a little hole away from the other graves. Bury your doll, black cloth and all, and add the black candle drippings and ashes from the Black Arts incense. Pour a small amount of urine over the grave in an equal-armed cross (the four directions) pattern. It is done. Turn your back and don't look behind you.

The results of these spells have been interesting. Harassers have made sudden mistakes and brought themselves down; they have gotten fired, exposed, sued, or divorced. Some rapists we did this spell against had serious car accidents and ended up in the hospital; others got caught in the act and were sentenced to long jail terms. None has escaped their Nemesis.

3. Organize!   The biggest problem for the working woman today is isolation. You work, and then you go home. On weekends you try to catch up on your life. Monday comes, and you pick up the routine. In order to stimulate your awareness of collective female consciousness, you need to join a group in which women can feel safe speaking their minds. Seek out a consciousness-raising group (call your local chapter of NOW) or organize one yourself. It takes only a small group of friends and a commitment to meet once a week to talk about a topic relating to your lives.

There are only a few rules, such as letting each woman have an equal opportunity to talk and not judging or trashing each other. No interruption or advice need be given. You pick a topic for each session and stick to it. Participating in such a group will make you realize how many things you share with other women, how in your troubles you are not alone. This realization breaks your isolation and empowers you to use your will. The group can also evolve into an action group to address an issue publicly. Part of exercising your will is using the political power of your vote.

Meditation: The Wild Woman Shows You What You Really Need

It's time for another visit to the source of your power, your wildness. Last time that you met with Wild Woman, you promised to come back soon. You should always keep your word to your Wild Woman. But when you go journeying in the inner world, you should have a purpose. This time, your purpose is to find out about needs you have suppressed for so long you no longer know they are there.

Do you remember how she said to get in touch with her most quickly? Was it by holding a necklace your mother gave you, by rubbing a green stone? Recall here what your Wild Woman told you. If you don't remember, reach her by taking a little more time to travel back to the place where you met her using the same procedure you followed before.

Breathe into your toes, wiggling them and relaxing them. Follow with breaths to your legs and hips and chest and arms and neck and face and brain, each time relaxing another part of the body. Now, move your energy from your brain to that safe place where things are moist and woodsy, where the mountains are high and wrapped in clouds, and the gods are near.

Look for the Wild Woman. What is she up to? Is she hiding? Is she back in her cavern? Or is she dancing among the trees? Sense her and make another contact. She is our unseen body, our life energy, our nature. We have to develop a conscious relationship with her in order to raise our self-esteem and strengthen our immune systems, but we must do it out of compassion for this wise animal self.

That sweet beast within us has been doing her best, surviving for millions of years, evolving, enduring, and coming down through our genes into the present. The immense spirit of the earth has split into millions of pieces, and each of us has part of that precious whole. When we gather together, more parts of her are given shape, and so her form emerges. But you can do the same thing, a bit more slowly, by working alone.

Find your Wild Woman now.

Give her greetings and a gift. She has a childlike spirit, and presents will always put her in a more cooperative mood. The miracle of this is that you need only to reach into your magic basket, and you will pull out the appropriate gift. Give it to her and observe her. See what she wants you to do.

Is she in need of a good scrub and combing? Is she in the mood to walk with you? You can learn a great deal just walking through the woods, watching her shift shapes, posing questions, and listening to her answers. Today ask her to point to the place on her body where your energy is getting stuck. What part of your body needs more help? Look within for a minute to feel it, too.

When she has told you what she needs, thank her and depart slowly, riding on your breath like a bird on the breeze. Breathe so that your awareness focuses in your own face. With another breath, imagine yourself back in your own neck, shoulders, arms, chest, hips, legs, and finally toes, until you have slipped completely back into your body. Wiggle your toes. Open your eyes. Relax and ground.

You have made your second journey to meet your Wild Woman, but what did it mean? What you have "seen" in this internal journey is an important message for the rest of your body and soul. The unseen body is part of the seen body, but we have suppressed the senses that would let us check it out as easily as we do our muscles and skin. Identifying a pain in your physical body tells you where tension is settling or where a muscle has been strained. The sensations of the unseen body are a symbolic language to get in touch with other needs. By indicating some part of her body, the Wild Woman has told you where you need to send your energy to heal yourself or even just to prevent an energy drain.

The skills you learn in your inner life will save your outer life every time. Read and meditate on the meaning of your Wild Woman's hurt and do something about it. Spend energy in a positive way, no matter what that might be. Draw a picture of the way she wants to be on paper and color it. Make it out of clay. Open your mind to finding ways to meet the need she has made you aware of. Let this inner voice of the Wild Woman continue to speak within you and follow her lead.

★ ★ ★

Wednesday

★ ★ ★ ★ ★ ★ ★ ★ ★ ★ ★

Communicate by Putting Your Wits to Work

Wednesday's Energy

On Wednesdays you should do your organizing for the next week. Make long-term and short-term plans, plot your strategies, write up what needs to be written, make phone calls, follow up, and be your intellectual self all day long. You should also begin thinking about your weekend plans.

Trend predictors and futurists all say the Information Age is coming. Women have always been considered to be naturally better at communicating than men, so this should be a golden opportunity for us to shine. It has been predicted that women will make great advances in the workplace and break the glass ceiling that has kept us from fully realizing our potential. Girls master speech earlier in their lives than boys; we use language more often to project our ideas and wills and use our ideas and wills more creatively than men. We also read more. We are the bestseller makers, the magazine consumers, the novel readers, the self-help book consumers. We watch the media more. Women are the natural heirs of the communication power in the universe.

It's Wednesday: Start Communicating

Wednesday is Woden's day, named by the Anglo-Saxons after Woden (the Norse Odin), the Germanic god of magic, battle fury, poetic inspiration, and ecstasy. Odin is a shaman, and he appears sometimes as the god of wisdom and sometimes as a trickster. He is a god of consciousness and communication.

Odin wandered the worlds in search of knowledge, learning most often from women. He studied witchcraft with Freya, the Goddess of prosperity, love, and earth magic, and became a shaman. He was so thirsty for wisdom that he hanged himself from the Tree of Life upside down for nine days and nine nights without food or drink, himself sacrificed to himself, wounded by his own spear. When he had pushed himself to his limits, he became one with the pattern of the universe and drew from the chaos of the world the sacred runes.

Odin gave the runes to humans, elves, dwarfs, even giants—to anyone seeking knowledge. You have already encountered some of the runes in the spells in this book—they are the sacred alphabet of northern Europe whose symbols represent sounds, letters, and ideas. They can be used for writing or, like the Tarot cards, for divination.

In Greek and Roman mythology the closest equivalent to the wisdom/communication aspect of Odin was Mercury (in Greek, Hermes). The Romans assigned the planet Mercury, which governs intelligence and communication, to the week's middle day. Because of Mercury's wisdom, Wednesday governs intelligence and quick wit, teaching, adaptability, the ability to organize details and think in patterns and computers. Because Mercury is a wanderer (he was the messenger of the gods), it influences commuters, travelers for business or pleasure, and comings and goings.

Some say that before patriarchy Mercury the planet used to belong to Minerva, the gracious Goddess of wisdom, crafts, and sciences. Minerva is in charge of scripts, incorporations, contracts, licenses, proposals, plans, blueprints, and all manner of paperwork. She is in charge of traffic, the flow of information, travelers, telephones, and making connections. Like Mercury, she governs things of the mind, but she is also concerned with the nervous system and the health and growth of the young. She is the Goddess of the Information Age.

The Goddess Speaks: Sarasvati

Sarasvati, "the Flowing One," is the Goddess of communication in the Hindu pantheon of India. She is the daughter and partner of Brahma and represents the union of power and intelligence that allows creation to begin. Her power is that of creation through the word, and chief among her other names is Vach, "Speech." In that form, she is the wife of the god Vision and the mother of the Emotions. She also gives birth to the apsaras, who are celestial water nymphs who represent uncreated potentialities.

Sarasvati taught humans the arts of language and writing. For this reason, she is the Goddess of eloquence, wisdom, learning, arts, and music and the mother of poetry. She is a good patroness for women involved in any aspect of the literary profession, arts, or entertainment or anyone whose job includes a lot of writing.

Sarasvati is pictured as being very fair and graceful, wearing white or pale colors. She sits on a lotus and has a moon crescent on her brow. She may be shown playing the *vineh,* a long-necked stringed instrument whose vibrations set creation in motion, or with four arms holding a *vineh,* a book, a Hindu rosary, and an elephant hook. On her holiday, no one reads books or plays musical instruments. Instead, the inkwells are cleaned, placed on her altar, and worshiped as her shrines.

Pictures of Sarasvati can sometimes be purchased at stores that sell spices and other imported goods to the Indian community. However, you do not need a picture—a book, perhaps your journal, or a musical instrument will honor her as well. Burn sandalwood incense for her and make offerings of rice, fruit, or flowers. If you are working on a report, a book, or anything involving words, place your work on her altar overnight and ask for her help. Plans and sketches for other creative projects can be placed under her protection as well. Before you get up to make a presentation, an appeal to your boss for a raise, or anything requiring eloquence, say a quick prayer to Sarasvati.

Bring the presence of the Goddess into your life throughout the day. In the morning, hum, "Aum," and hail her as Gayatri, "Protector of Vital Energies." Ask that you may know the immensity of creation and be guided by her divine power through the day. At noon, hail her as Savitri, "Hymn to the Sun." On your lunch break, go out where you can feel the warmth of the sun and hum the sound "ooooh." Let her radiant light flow into you and fill you until you feel as if you are glowing. Ask her to clarify your thinking, to kindle new ideas within you, and to let her wisdom shine so brightly through you that it will be apparent to all. At sunset, honor the goddess as Sarasvati, "the Flowing One," and softly hum the sound "aim." In Hindu tradition, the "ai" represents the Goddess, and the "m" is the removal of pain. As you make this sound, feel the stress of the day flowing out of you and take in knowledge and wisdom, mastery over words, and the power of speech.

Wednesday's Scent

Wednesday's scent is rosemary oil. It stimulates memory, love, and the conscious mind. It has been said that smelling rosemary often will keep you young.

Wednesday's Gems

Get some green stones, *malachite, green turquoise,* or *jade.* Keep them in a small bowl on your desk, and each day, when you come to work, visualize money, contracts, commissions accumulating on your desk mingled with your green stones. Please refer to Wednesday's spells to see how you can put your gems to work for you.

Wednesday's Color

Yellow is a manifesting color. This color is good for enhancing your communication with others. You are heard better in yellow.

Depression is held at bay, and you can present your skill and ideas with more success. If you are asking for a raise, wear yellow.

Wearing *white* reduces muscular tension. It is a good color to wear when you have to meditate, mediate, teach, or heal somebody. A woman in white suggests focus and purity of thought and actions. It signals positive thinking, openness to new ways, but also a willingness to get rid of nonessentials. Use it when you want others to trust you. However, white, like black, may work better in smaller doses. Dressing completely in white may make you appear pure to the point of being unapproachable.

Silver stimulates self-respect and invokes the spirituality of the moon. This color reduces inner fears, always a good idea. Metallic colors in large doses are not usually considered appropriate for the office, but you can wear them as accents and of course as jewelry.

Gold stimulates prosperity consciousness. It is a color of self-reward and enhances feelings of security. It motivates you to set high goals. Gold is a good color for fashion consultants, princesses, and queens.

Humming for Power

The communication center of the body is in the throat. Although the throat provides the volume for speech, it can also be a source of pure, nonverbal sound. Nonverbal communication is the kind the Wild Woman does best. In the office, especially if you are alone, you can do some humming as you work. It enhances your brain work and calms your nerves. If your phone voice is too thin, humming deeply will create more resonance in your voice and make it more pleasing.

When witches meet and raise power, we hum. This kind of humming is a sonic meditation in which you vibrate your skull and brain with your lips closed. Doing this for about three minutes will put you into an altered state of consciousness. If you want to tune up your brain, you can hum to yourself at work. Hum for a few moments before starting work. Hum before performing spells.

The humming vibration wakes up your brain cells and makes you receptive to information carried on the winds. Through humming in a ceremonial circle, you learn nonverbally how each person in the circle is feeling. We also receive healing from each other on this vibrational level. We all feel stronger after we have hummed together. The colors we see are brighter, time slows down, we perceive reality differently, and we are calmer, more open to healing work.

Clearly, humming could be a good way to tune yourself up for a day at the office. But how do you do it?

Before beginning magical work, I always teach women how to raise power by vibrating their brains. The most common mistake women make is to let the energy of the sound get stuck in their noses or foreheads, or even in the throat itself. Learning to move this energy upward into the top of the head is the first lesson. You can try it right now—place your hand on the top of your head and vibrate your vocal cords gently without strain. If you feel your crown vibrate with your hand you are doing it right. Humming as a spiritual exercise provides both rhythm and entertainment. When the wave forms resonate together, they amplify each individual contribution and magnify it into one great resonant sound. Sometimes when I hum together with sixty or so women, I feel totally carried away on the wave of the sound, washed and purified, even if it is a group that is creating this sonic resonance for the first time. "Maaa," we chant. The first sound is *Ma*, Mother.

When the chanting is done well, you cannot tell where your voice begins and others end. The sound takes on a life of its own. It instructs and rises and falls spontaneously; it has components of discord and harmonies, but they come out together in a beautiful great tapestry of sound. We teach this kind of meditation as an improvisational technique because vibration/meditation/prayer ought to come directly from the individual's heart/throat/brain.

Spells for Communication

Spells for powerful speech begin with the telephone. When the phone rings, you are doing business. Your voice will convey what mood you are in, what your expectations are, and what you are afraid of, even when all you have said is "hello." Because the vibrations of your brain have an effect on the person at the other end of the line, it's best if your mind and psyche are at peace with your work.

Always take a few deep breaths before you make important calls. Repeat silently, "All my needs are easily met."

If you are negotiating something, whether you are creating a product or delivering an item, be sure that you communicate clearly the basic information who, what, when, and how much.

1. Entraining

Sometimes communication has a dimension that goes beyond facts or even words. This is what Kay Gardner (in *Soundscapes*) calls *entrainment*. Oh, my Goddess, what does that mean? This is an all-important concept, and *Webster's* isn't much help in defining it.

Let me explain through a story.

I was giving a workshop in Germany and having some difficulties with the language, because although I used to speak German in high school and still understand it, I now need a translator to help me teach in German. I was trying to make the workshop participants into a unit, to get them to all resonate to the silent beat of the universe. The group included people from Holland, England, Denmark, and Sweden, with some Yugoslavians and Hungarians as well. And it wasn't working. I was speaking as well as I could, but the audience was not with me. They were too involved catching the meaning, the phrase, the substance, to pick up on the emotional and psychic significance. This went on for a while, until I got very nervous and started speaking faster and faster. When the translator begged for time, I threw my hands up and called a recess. By this time our collective vibration was at its most shrill pitch.

During the recess I started singing without words, just expressing my feelings. When we gathered together after the recess I used this toning as a device to bring in the members of the group one by one as they too sang their feelings without words. At last there came a moment when we all sang beautifully together, creating a sound that was resonant, rich, unified. We had achieved entrainment.

After this I could calmly begin again, and everything they had missed before now became easy and clear. Nobody took notes any more; they trusted that they would get it, and they did. Ever since then, I never start a workshop with words but always begin with humming or singing, an entrainment activity of some sort.

Communication is a dance with its own rhythms. You join that dance by communicating. Listening is also dancing to the rhythms. When you are a good listener, you become part of the speaker. The sound of her voice, the vibrations of her psyche, all affect you physically, emotionally, mentally, and even chemically. Entrainment is being in rhythm with our activity, with our surroundings, with the universe.

How can you have entrainment with co-workers in a business situation? Here are some things to try.

Eating and drinking together are one way to draw together. Having music softly playing in the background in your office is another. Find a common ground for conversation. Taking an interest in each other's private lives and interests is a way of establishing communication. Try lighting a small purple candle for the harmony.

Once this link is established, you can talk to your co-workers about impending work, commitments, or help you may need from them. Once you are in entrainment, you have a chance to get what you need. Your fellow workers will hear you.

In psychic work we pay attention to the vibrational nature of all things. This kind of communication expands our existing state of consciousness and organizes it. In order to have a future, we have to communicate. As Anodea Judith says in *Wheels of Life,* "Communications interface the past and the present and create the future." She defines *communication* as the naming and organizing of consciousness for the purpose of transmitting and propagating itself. The essence of communication is creativity. In altering our patterns of communication, we become creators, creating the reality and future of our lives during each and every second.

2. Silence, the Deep Pond's Secret

Sometime when you can control whether you are alone or not, try *not* speaking aloud for a whole day. Allow yourself to listen, to be aware of the vibrations around you. As an exercise, try entraining animals and plants without words. Enter their minds and bodies with your consciousness and become them. Walk in the woods and lean against trees, pressing against their trunks with your spine. Then enter the tree from the bottom up and travel inside it. You will know when you have managed this. The tree will become real to you as never before. You will see the sap rising; you will hear the tree talking to you. If you have a pet, practice with your animal, who is already in entrainment with you. Talk to your animal silently to see if she will respond.

3. Bach Essences to Help with Communication

Gorse essence is a remedy for those who have lost faith or hope. You cannot communicate when you are depressed, so take a few drops of gorse to heal the illness in the emotional body that has prevented you from raising your hopes. Hope is essential for mental health.

For freshness and vitality of the mind, use a few drops of *hornbeam*. This essence is good for enhancing communication. It builds up the mental energy you need to continue a task you set out to do but got too tired to complete.

Cerato is a flower that relates to the inner voice, to certainty and intuition. Those of us who cannot trust our intuition or our vibrational wisdom and need some external authority to provide our reality need to take this Bach remedy.

4. When the Computer Is Down or Won't Behave

This spell comes from my friend Laurel, an office witch. She loves the runes for magic in the office because runes make the life force available to you. The computer is a device for powerful thinking, so she uses the rune Ansuz ᚨ. This is the rune of intellect, inspiration, and communication. This rune is associated with the Norse god Odin, who was a god of wisdom, wanderer between the worlds, giver of the runes and the power of using words in poetry.

Next Laurel uses the rune Sowilo ᛋ. This is the symbol of the sun and the sun path, that which nature requires. Seeking after wholeness is the heart of the sacred warrior's quest. Sowilo is regeneration, recharging, self-repair, and victory.

Finally Laurel uses Elhaz ᛉ, the rune of protection. Elhaz represents the curved horns of the elk.

Laurel draws these three symbols on her dark computer screen with her saliva, her essence. Visualizing the symbols and the images they represent, she links them to the machine and actually endows it with a spirit she can talk to.

5. A Spell for Giving a Speech

To help your thoughts flow freely, burn a yellow candle and meditate on your ideas. Candles that come in a glass jar and burn for a week are great. As long as they are somewhere they can't be knocked over, they can be left to burn (although it is a good idea to place them in a dish or saucer just in case the glass cracks). Some people leave theirs burning in the bathtub. Once lit, the candles burn for seven days and delight you with their yellow fire dance.

Burn purple candles when you write, give a speech, or have a big meeting or conference. If you can get away with having this candle on the conference table, it will entrain your staff into unity. The mere presence of a single candle burning in the conference room creates powerful vibrations that will beneficially affect your co-workers. It will awaken their spiritual selves, making the work go better, faster, and with more humanity.

6. Getting a Raise

Perform this spell on a new moon or a waxing moon.

Anything having to do with money is anxiety producing. You have to change the way *you* have been thinking about it. You deserve more money for the work you are

doing; in fact, they should have given it to you long ago. That raise is already rightfully yours. Do you believe this? You must now plant this idea in the head of the money man.

Visualize your boss saying "yes" a lot. Wear green clothes, think green, do green things such as gardening, touching the earth, being in the green. If you need to submit a written request for more money, rub lavender on it. Wear lavender oil as your perfume.

Buy a green candle and write the name of your boss on it along with the answer you want: "Yes (your name), we want to give you a raise." Specify the amount of raise you expect.

Set up a green altar. You can use a green tablecloth with green leaves and flowers in decoration, your green stones for the centerpiece, and the green candle. Anoint the green candle with bergamot. By now you wouldn't dare to be without bergamot oil, would you? Burn the candle nine nights in a row, fifteen to thirty minutes each night, and visualize your checkbook balance getting larger and larger. Visualize your boss saying yes to you; visualize money-producing ideas coming home. Burn some money-drawing incense (available at occult supply stores), which is green, and say:

> Money that is needed,
> Money that is speeded,
> Money that is mine,
> Come! Now is the time!

Repeat this nine times each night.

When you have finished the spell, collect the remnants from the altar (wax drippings, wilted flowers, incense ashes) and cast them into a living body of water, such as an ocean, a river, or a lake. After throwing the remnants in the water, turn your back and walk away without looking back.

Wait a moon and then ask confidently for a raise. The Goddess in the office will provide.

7. A Hex on Troubles

Note that before you do this spell you should be very sure that a takeover of your company by someone else would in fact cause destruction and disaster rather than saving it from mismanagement, bankruptcy, or the like. The office rumor mill can grind out some pretty fantastic stories. Take a little time to investigate any tales you hear and be sure that your own management is telling you the truth about what is going on. As in all magic, you should have all the facts and consider all possible consequences before taking on the karma of hexing. If you attack the innocent, the hex returns to you threefold. However, if you are not attacking the innocent, you are entitled to defend yourself safely.

If you have company troubles, such as the threat of a corporate takeover, burn a black candle. Write the name of the aggressor backward three times on the candle. Project into it all the problems and visualize the takeover collapsing.

If you are fighting for your financial life, it is worth a more elaborate spell. Prepare an altar with black cloth. Gather a few dried bones or use a picture of a skull—anything to make you feel this is the labor of destruction. Represent your own company by a color that you feel is appropriate, maybe something from the color scheme of the office or from your logo. Represent the takeover bullies by a black candle, which you anoint first with vinegar, then roll in an herb called *stinging nettle*. Your own company candle should be anointed with your own saliva and rolled in cinnamon, which stands for money.

Now place the two candles on the altar table, the distance between them depending on how close the danger is. Light a dispelling incense such as Black Arts or a purifying incense such as sage.

Light the candle representing your company and say, "This is our company, our livelihood, our place of business." Tell the Goddess the story as briefly and concisely as you can. Then light the black candle representing the company attempting the takeover and say, "Here is the enemy entity." Once more, explain the problem.

Now move the enemy candle a little farther away from your company's candle and say:

> I send (name) away from mine and me.
> I send them to the bottom of the sea.
> I send them to the pit of hell,
> Where they can taste their evil power well.

Repeat this spell every evening for five nights in a row, moving the enemy company's candle a little farther away from your company's candle each time. Visualize the enemy getting in trouble with the law. Visualize them failing. On the fifth night place the candles as far apart as possible. You may even take the black candle out of the room and let it finish burning in the bathtub. When it is finished burning, it is best to bury the remnants, thereby burying all future threats.

On the following night, light a white candle next to your company candle on the altar in thanks. Take your own candle drippings and throw them in a living body of water. When you have done this, turn around and don't look back.

Don't talk about this spell to anybody who was not working it with you; talking about the spell can weaken it. Your secrecy will be a vessel for its power.

To amplify the effect, draw the rune Hagalaz ᚻ , which stands for disruptive change, on top of the rune Othalaz ᛟ , which stands for home and property, so that any plans the corporate officers intending the takeover might have for making themselves at home in your space would be extremely disrupted. You might add Tyr ᛏ , the rune of justice, or Raidho ᚱ , because it means "the right path" in certain contexts, to your own candle to make things work out.

Wednesday Meditation: Wild Woman Communicates

Come now to visit with the Wild Woman as she is presiding in her temple of the Wild Things. She is no longer the shy wild creature we met earlier. She has found her center and now possesses the awe-inspiring power of the spirits.

She is the Sibyl, the Pythia, the Völva, the Prophetess. She sits with legs spread wide apart over a deep chasm in the earth, a memory of a recent earthquake. She is not afraid. Below her in the crack of the good earth burns sweet-smelling sandalwood mixed with kephi incense, the finest offered. Her eyes are closed. You approach her with reverence.

Your whole body is relaxed as you breathe deeply the amber incense you are burning. There are others in this temple with you, women and men all waiting for the moment when the priestess, the Wild Woman, looks into your eyes and asks you, "Show me your heart, child."

It is almost your turn now, and suddenly it is. The priestess is totally focused on you. Her eyes deeply penetrate your soul.

With your right hand you take your heart, with your whole life and all your feelings, and hand it over to her warm, capable hands. Feel her careful handling. She receives your heart and kisses it, and all the hurt from your emotional body just melts away. Now she is going to say something to you. You wait, and watch her face. Listen carefully. The message can be short or long. Remember what was said.

She hands your heart back to you and you place it in your body again. You kiss her hands in gratitude as you would kiss the hands of a benefactor. You are now moving into the back of the temple and allowing others to speak to her. You feel unconditional love.

The future is constantly changing, as we are changing. What you glimpse through prophecy is true only for that phase of time. Dance your dance of life and don't hesitate or get hung up on the future.

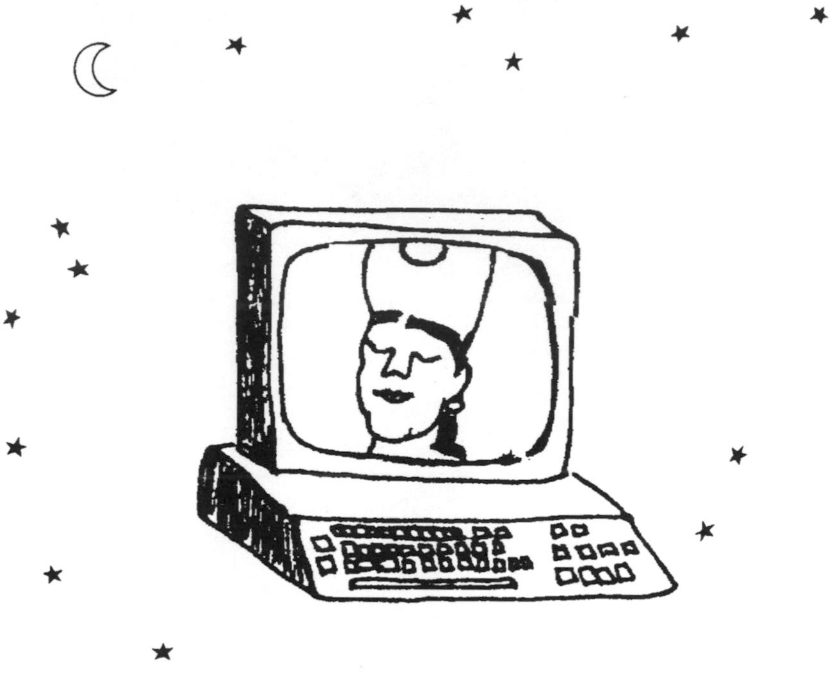

Thursday

* ★ ★ ★ ★ ★ ★ ★ ★ ★ ★ ★

The Rule of the Heart

Thursday's Energy

Thursday is the "slide" day—you've made it through most of the week, and now you're on the downslope to the weekend! On this day you should start seeing the results of the things you've been working on. It is a day for organizing, but it is also a time to share the results with others. After work on Thursday is the best time for you to do your grocery shopping.

Thursday's Meaning

Thursday is Thor's day, named after the huge and hearty Norse god who defends the world from the forces of chaos with his hammer of thunder. In the old days Thor was the most popular of the gods because he was the one you could depend on for help and protection. Not only was he the great defender, but he could also calm a storm or bring the welcome rain.

In the Mediterranean, the thunder god was Jupiter (in Greece, Zeus), who was also the ruler of Olympus. Before patriarchy rewrote mythology, Juno, his queen, was associated with Thursday. She was the Lady of Cities, the great organizer. She ruled marriages, relationships, child raising, and civic law. All these values belong to Thursday. Whether you are looking at Thor, who guards the perimeter between the ordered world of human society and the wilderness, or at Jupiter, reigning over Olympus, or at Juno, the queen whose domain is the sacred center of the city or of the home, the powers of Thursday have to do with protection, order, and sovereignty. However, the rule of Juno is based not only on law but also on love.

Picture Juno as a tall matron. She wears the mural crown of the walled city on her head and holds the scepter of sovereignty in her right hand and a child in the other. Familiar? Of course. Many official buildings built in the classic style feature this image of the Goddess. You have seen her on the fronts of museums, law buildings, and even banks!

To Thursday belong the jovial qualities of expansiveness, optimism, mercy, generosity, success, protection, and philanthropy. The planet Jupiter is called the "bringer of joy." It rules over those in authority, especially leaders, judges, executives and administrators, the professional classes in general, long-distance travel, business and commerce, universities, animals, wisdom, and even gambling.

A Goddess for Thursday: Kwan Yin: Love, Higher Intelligence, and Mercy

If you walk through Chinatown in any city, you will see statues of Kwan Yin everywhere—in grocery stores, pastry shops, and restaurants. She is seated on a lotus throne in regal repose, dressed in long, flowing robes with flowers in her hand. Kwan Yin is the Asian Lady of Compassion. She represents love, mercy, and higher intelligence. Her name comes originally from Nu Kwa, Earth Woman, the spirit of the earth. The Buddhists identified her with a holy woman who refused release from the wheel of reincarnation in order to remain in contact with the creatures of the world to protect and help them.

Kwan Yin is said to be always ready to aid whosoever calls to her. This is especially impressive because her stories are not all old legends. There have been many recent sightings and stories about people she has rescued at sea and on the land. I once met a woman who told me how as a child in China she suffered from pneumonia and all the village medicines couldn't help her. Her mother went to the old shrine of Kuan Yin asking for help. The voice in the cave (usually a devotee of the Goddess who served the temple), told her to tell her story to the first man she met on her way home. Now this was rural China, and the mother had slim hopes of meeting anyone. But as it happened, she did see someone—a young white doctor. He was the first man to bring penicillin into China, and when she told him her story, her daughter got the right medicine and lived to tell the tale. In China Kwan Yin is still very much revered and prayed to in cases of severe illness and by women desiring to conceive a healthy child. She is addressed as Merciful Mother.

Kwan Yin should have a statue in your office, especially if you are dealing with business from Asia. The traditional worship of Kwan Yin includes chanting and meditating. Light some Oriental incense when you begin; put out a few grains of wild rice or seven oranges for her. While you burn the incense, pray to her aloud or silently:

> Merciful Mother, please give me the ability to understand and accept people as you do. Allow me to communicate well my thoughts and let my purpose shine.

For more ideas on how to work with Kwan Yin, read my books *Grandmother of Time* and *Grandmother Moon*. To strengthen compassion within you, work for peace one day a month. Try to also work for the earth one day a month.

Thursday's Scent

Thursday's scent is *patchouli*. Oh dear, did I say the wrong thing? Everybody "hates" patchouli, or is it the memory of the synthetic scent that pervaded everybody's living room in the sixties that we'd like to forget? The true patchouli scent is a mental energizer. Wear just a little bit of it on your wrists or inhale its scent from your special bottle three times, and it will remind you of wildness, even help you to visualize your

Wild Woman at her morning chores. There will be mossy fields in your mind, and deep forests will awaken in your old memories. If you wear it to work, it may excite unwanted male attention, as men also start thinking of mossy fields and deep green forests and frolicking with you in the nude. Beware! But wear patchouli around a potential lover, and he or she will react with romantic thoughts and feelings.

Thursday's Gem

The stone of the self-mending heart is *rose quartz*. For the days when you are most sensitive or have been hurt emotionally, keep a big piece of rose quartz at hand and hold on to it. It is said to mend hurt feelings just by being around. I keep a piece of rose quartz on top of my computer to make me love writing on it more. It cheers me to look at it between paragraphs. You feel more patient and at ease when some rose quartz, however small or large the piece may be, is in your field of vision. Wearing rose quartz beads is also calming and helps you keep your perspective on things, and of course a necklace or bracelet or pin of rose quartz will make you look very attractive.

Thursday's Colors

Mauve, a shade that is almost purple, helps us to trust our feelings. It stimulates intuition, calms inner confusions, reduces overactivity. Mauve is a good color to wear if you are a boss; it will get cooperation from others.

79

Lavender is the ultimate in relaxation colors. Wear this, and everybody around you will feel that you are calm and collected. Use this color in high-stress situations when everybody else is losing his or her grip. If you are the director of a play, for example, wear it on opening night. Lavender is a great color to wear around children. It stimulates intellectual thought and enhances inner beauty.

Purple is the royal color of hard work, fame, and fortune. You appear regal in this color, and you will get more respect when wearing it. Spirituality and power are associated with purple. This is another good boss color; if you use it in your office, its effects will become associated with you in the eyes of your co-workers. However, if you are low on the totem pole, wearing too much purple may be seen as threatening.

Make Those Around You in the Office Feel Loved

You make your heart power grow when you radiate awareness of others' needs into the universe. This should be easy. Women are conditioned to regard other beings' needs more than our own. Create an environment where you can give and receive a lot of strokes. Strokes are authentic compliments.

Find opportunities to say things like this: "I really appreciated it, Sally, when you saved me a chair in the meeting so I could come late and not have to stand for two hours." "I really think you are generous, Mary, when you bring your cookies to the office parties." "You are so creative, Nancy!" "You are radiant today!" "You are doing a great job!" "Congratulations!"

Be a fountain of strokes, and you will find them coming back to you. Focusing your attention on your positive aspects stimulates the power center of the heart. It builds you up.

Tender, Loving Lunches

Mary told me that she was promoted to replace a male manager who had always rushed off with the other males to partake in power lunches. She expected to be asked herself when she took over, but the men didn't invite her. Power lunches were affirmations of men's privileges over the lower ranks (women) of workers. It is a ritual of bonding for the bosses to share the pleasure of eating together. Mary didn't qualify because she was seen as a member of a lower caste, women.

I suggested that she and her female co-workers form a TLC (tender, loving care) lunch group. She should set a time when all the females would disappear to their TLC lunch and let the men pale in envy. This would create a tradition that would immediately be seen as threatening to the male hierarchy. Why? Because male "one-upsmanship" works only if you play your role as "one down." If you elevate yourself so that your own needs will be met, you become an equal. The power lunches will sink in status to just another excuse to get drunk in the middle of the day. TLC implies that you get tender, loving care; it's a witness to your presence in the workforce and that you receive female approval—in other words, a true psychic value exchange.

At these TLC meetings each of the women can express appreciation for the others, give out "strokes" and receive them. Personal visiting and checking in with each other can follow. Sometimes TLC meetings can spawn rebellion, resistance, or new solutions to problems that may come up.

Thursday's Spells for the Heart

1. Spell to Stimulate Self-Love

When you wake up in the morning, light a little sage incense in your room, taking a few moments to inhale its wonderful purifying scent. Repeat to yourself three times while breathing in:

> I am the conductor of love in the universe.

Breathe out and say

> I am wonderful and beautiful!

Breathe in and repeat:

> I am the conductor of love in the universe!

Breathe out and say:

> I am receiving love from the universe!
> All my needs are easily met!

Play with this until you believe it. A spell is, after all, a prayer until it comes true. Then it is magic.

2. Mothering the Office

If you need to have everybody feel good and happy around you, you can do many witchy things to bend your reality.

When you keep wild flowers or roses on your desk, you animate mothering vibrations. Wearing rose oil on your skin will make everybody relax and feel that you care about them. Do not use the normal synthetic chemical perfumes. Use natural oils; they cost more but last a lot longer and have beneficial psychic effects.

Bake cookies with vanilla powder to promote a sense of safety, home, and caring. When you need to calm the collective nerves of your co-workers and get people on your side, mother them with chocolate, cocoa drinks, and fresh-cut flowers placed where all can see.

3. Pink Mist Visualization

When you enter your workplace, imagine a huge pink bubble in which the computers and the people are working. When somebody enters your office, pink mist them with your heart power and watch them react with a friendlier attitude. If you can, buy a nice lump of rose quartz at a rock or curio shop. In your office, look at it for a while or just hold it, absorbing its rosy glow, and take that energy into your heart.

The visualization is that you are blowing a pink mist from your heart that develops into a huge bubble. Once the bubble is in place, tell it to stay around the office even while you are working at other things. This is something for the Wild Woman to do, since she certainly isn't watching your left brain activities.

4. Birthdays at the Office

The celebration of birthdays is a ritual that is already well established in the workplace. Contribute gladly to this effort, with thoughtful cards and sweet treats. If possible, invite the birthday girl out with the rest of you to a group luncheon at which you can order a birthday cake with candles.

The celebration of storytelling and eating should go together. Therefore, rather than having the birthday woman blow out the candles, ask her to tell the story of her life as she lights the candles, remembering the years one by one. This is the true ritual. A good way to prompt her for stories is to say something like this: "Okay, so now you've got to age seventeen. Who did you love back then?" And the funny stories will tumble out like precious gems from a treasure box.

5. Saying Goodbye

Another ritual that is often practiced in healthy offices is a goodbye party when somebody leaves or is "let go." It is healing to get together and perform a little magic before you say goodbye. Here is a witchy version of the same.

Take some gold dust (pyrite), place it in the hand of the person who is leaving, and let her blow it to the four corners of the universe (east, south, west, and north) with a wish for the future. When she has finished, you should all chime in with your blessings and confirm her wishes. For example, it might go as follows.

Woman (blowing to the east): "May I find profitable employment with good benefits, stability, and opportunities for promotion!"

All: "It is done! It is done! It is done!"

Woman (blowing to the south): "May I find a job that will use my passion!"

All: "It is done! It is done! It is done!"

Woman (blowing to the west): "May I find a new job that will give my heart satisfaction!"

All: "It is done! It is done! It is done!"

Woman (blowing to the north): "May Mother Earth be healed and may my work never harm her!"

All: "It is done! It is done! It is done!"

When it's all finished, party together as usual.

6. Spell for a New Lover (New Moon)

A well-loved worker is a happy worker.

When you feel you have healed and are ready to date again, write your name on a pink candle three times and place it on your altar at home. Your altar can be any space where you can safely burn a candle—the top of your bureau, a space on a bookshelf, a mantel, or a window ledge. What matters is that the altar be beautiful to you. Keep it uncluttered and free of other items such as money or keys. Set your pink candle on the altar and light it. Collect some rose petals and sprinkle them in a circle around the candle. As you drop rose petals to the east of your candle, say, "I call from the east the new lover who will be right for me. Like a wind you awaken; like a wish you now rise! Come into my life!"

Sprinkle rose petals to the south of your candle and say, "From the south I conjure the new lover who will be right for me. Enter my life with fire and love; enter my life with joy and dance."

Sprinkle to the west and say, "From the west, Aphrodite's corner, I conjure the new lover who will be right for me. You are carried to me by the tides of the sea. Enter my life; I have opened the door."

Finally, to the north sprinkle rose petals, saying, "From the north I call you, new lover who will be right for me. From the earth you rise; you come to me quickly; you come to me wise. I have opened the door to my heart, and now I call you forth. Materialize, oh, my lover; the Goddess wills it now."

A moon must go by before a spell is accomplished. After a moon has passed, you will begin to get results. You will meet new people, they will ask you out, and you must say yes. A love spell cast is a call to the universe to send you candidates for affection, and you must be polite enough to screen the applicants.

7. *Spell Against a Broken Heart*

One cannot work well when suffering from a broken heart. If you do not heal your emotional body, it will surely affect your physical body with headaches, colds, or various other discomforts. These are all physical metaphors of an unhappy heart.

If you have been very disappointed, if you have broken up with a loved one and feel lonely and betrayed, do this little spell. Get oil of lily (again, not the chemical synthetic but the real thing). Put it on a small cotton ball, place it in your hand, go to a window, and look at the moon, waxing or waning.

Now inhale the scent of lily from the cotton ball warmed by your hand and say to yourself:

> I am never alone.
> I am surrounded by the love of the Divine Mother,
> the Lady of the woods and the springs and the
>   flowers.
> I am never forlorn,
> For I am loved by the Divine Mother,
> And she has already sent her blessings after me,
> I am never alone or forlorn.
> My ancestors' spirits watch over me.
> I am beloved and blessed forever and beyond.

87

When you inhale the scent, take your time. Don't rush this spell.

You may want to wear lily scent all day to remind you of who you are. This is a good scent for those who have trouble showing their feelings and sharing them with others or asking for help. The lily is the special flower of the Goddess, surviving into modern times as the Blessed Virgin's sacred symbol.

Spells for Good Business

8. Wealth Spell on a Place of Business

Basil has a very beneficial scent. It lifts the spirits and makes you feel safe and invigorated. In ancient times it was used to clear the troubled mind.

You can benefit from simply crushing a basil leaf and inhaling it to sweep your mind clean. To bring money into a place of business, you have to appease the Wild Woman collective instinct, which is very fond of pesto, so do this spell.

Soak basil in a bowl of water for a day, then take the herb and use it to sprinkle water into all the corners and show windows, your cash register, and so on, saying:

> Basilia, Goddess of Wealth and Luck,
> Lift up all my desires to you
> And send them back with your golden touch.

If you cannot do this openly every day, do it once a month at the new moon. The scent of basil will please everybody, and it will energize the whole office. Keep a pot of basil growing in the window and let its scent freely float about; it will make the customers relax and shop. In a conference room the same procedure can be used, and remember that people whose moods and spirits are high will be agreeable and creative.

9. A Remedy Against Too Much Zeal

The Bach flower essence *vervain* is good for healing the tired soul who is always working for the good of all. If you feel you have to save the world today, and you also feel that nobody else is doing their part but you, and you are working so hard at it that you are losing your grip on your own life, calm down with three drops of vervain three times a day. Vervain, which is sacred to the Goddess of love, refuels the weary heart and gives perspective and a glad glow. When taking the three drops of vervain, think, "Mother, I bless you for holding us all in your lap securely."

Feel the weight lift and liberate your heart.

10. To Make a Good Impression at Interviews and Presentations

A wonderful smelling herb called *lemon balm* is credited with making its wearer appear beloved and agreeable to those who see her for the first time. You may wear lemon balm as an oil or a leaf sewn into your garment, or you can simply put a small amount in a little cloth bag in your pocket.

Lemon balm is associated with Juno/Jupiter, the planet of increase, wealth, and success. Think as you smell it, "Goddess, bless me as I shine and succeed."

Inhale this scent to calm down if you are very angry.

11. Money Cookies

One way to stay on the money path is by making magical food. There are a number of herbs associated with wealth that you can use in your own food or to feed others. Prosperity is one of those things that increases when it is shared. The more money your company makes, the better your chance for a bonus or a raise. Work for yourself and others at the same time.

For instance, look up a cookie recipe that calls for lots of cinnamon, a spice symbolic of money. Try cinnamon rolls or cinnamon bread. If you don't want to bake, buy something ready-made. Whether you start from scratch or augment store-bought baked goods, the spell is the same. Burn a green candle in the kitchen while you are preparing the magical food.

Break up a cinnamon stick and put it into a grinder. As you turn the handle, visualize your own finances or those of your employer steadily improving—imagine a healthy balance sheet, a bigger paycheck, contracts, smiling customers coming into the store—whatever images will indicate that business is booming. When the image is firmly established and clear, say:

As wealth* I give, so shall I live;
What goes around will come around.
These herbs I grind by power of mind,
What I have ground, by will be bound.

---

* Other words, such as health, love, and so on, can be substituted here, depending on the purpose for which you are grinding the herbs.

Continue humming and visualizing your desired result until the cinnamon is ground to powder. Then use it in your recipe or sprinkle it over the top of the baked goods you have bought. Eat the cookies yourself to improve your own finances, enjoying their rich, spicy flavor. Share them at coffee breaks to make everyone successful and to give your workplace a shot in the arm.

If the problem is at the top, bake special treats for the boss with cinnamon, ginger, allspice, cloves, basil, or dill. Give your boss a pair of green candles for his or her birthday. The main thing when you bake or cook for money is to visualize your wish as a completed fact. It isn't a wish anymore; it is already done!

The spell is the same for other purposes—just substitute different words and visualizations. Instead of a higher paycheck, you might visualize a promotion or visualize yourself handling cases and situations that a new job would entail.

12. A Spell for Cooperation

Here's something you can do to get more cooperation from others—co-workers, babysitters, bosses, and the like.

Try the time-honored food magic—feed the whole office blessed cookies you have baked. The traditional spices are vanilla, nutmeg, clover, and cinnamon. Any of these spices will carry your message if you put your energy into them by grinding them, stirring them, breathing on them, or holding your hand over them as you pronounce the spell.

> Warm hearts, warm seeds,
> My friends will help me meet my needs.
> My world is full of those who give.
> I get the help I need to live!

Visualize your co-workers acting positively toward you and your needs being met.

To increase the effect, sprinkle sugar in the shape of the runes Mannaz ᛗ and Ehwaz ᛖ over the cookies while they are still warm from the oven. Mannaz is the people rune, governing kinship, while Ehwaz, the horse rune, strengthens partnerships. Used together, they will encourage those who eat the cookies to work harmoniously together and with you. You might also use Wunjo ᚹ , the joy rune, and Fehu ᚠ , the rune of prosperity, to make these "relationships" joyous and fruitful.

Now take the cookies to the office and place them next to the coffee pot, so all that your co-workers can have some. If the office is big, you might attach a note saying who the cookies are from so that you will get the credit. Share cookies made in this way with anyone whose cooperation you need.

Thursday Meditation: The Wild Woman, Wild Lover

Your Wild Woman understands loving very well. She doesn't need to sleep through the day if there is passion (or even a nice, warm affection) around. When you are trying to make your office a more loving place, include her in the action. Send love to her and remember the feeling of love she has given you. Add a tiny heart, or a heart-shaped candy, to the nest you have made for her.

Spend a few moments gazing at the picture you have put up for her power place. Visualize her moving through it, stopping to enjoy and celebrate each tree and flower. See her stepping out of the picture and moving through your workplace. Your co-workers can't see her, but she is giving one a cheering pat on the back and blowing a little magic at another. Then she comes back to you and fills you with energy and ideas.

Is this all your imagination? Of course. But wait and see what happens. With the Wild Woman's power in you, you will have the energy to do a hundred little things that will cheer the place up. Don't drain yourself to do this. You don't have to worry about using up your own resources giving out all this love. Love is one of those things that gets stronger the more you use it. The power comes from your Wild Woman; all you have to do is let it flow through you.

On Thursday, whenever you have a little time before work or after work, or even sitting in traffic, close your eyes and breathe deeply, nine times, mentally walking down the mossy path that leads to the safe place where you last saw your Wild Woman. Allow your thoughts to empty; let her image emerge on its own, and allow it to appear in whatever shape or performing whatever activity she may desire.

Ah, there she is . . . sitting under a tree picking flowers out of her coat, lazy and happy. She is greeting you with her arms outstretched; you embrace her and smell her wild scent. She wants quality time. She wants to smooch.

Imagine that your Wild Woman is your favorite pet. Lie down with her and sing her a tune—in your safe world you can sing like a nightingale. Scratch her back or, better yet, give her a bath. Imagine her lathering up with herbal suds, as you delight in her animal pleasure (this mental exercise can be combined with your own morning bathing).

Then, in the middle of this pastoral scene, ask your Wild Woman what her heart desires. It is always a challenge to pop a question in the middle of a meditation and trust that there will be an answer. She could say, "I want more of you!" This means your self-love needs more work. But whatever she says, always reward her with embraces and promises of more good times together. And remember, these are promises that you must keep. Then say goodbye, assuring her that you will be back after work. Keep the mental doors open to your Wild Woman's reality.

96

Friday

Pleasure Day

Friday's Energy

It's the end of the week, and your Wild Woman knows that as soon as you leave your office she will be let out to play. You may already have lined up some activities, and your life is about to burst into full reality. Your work week is almost done, and ahead lies some playtime. Already you can enjoy the anticipation. Whether or not you have a date or family duties, your Wild Woman will demand that at least part of this time be dedicated to her. Even if your laundry has been growing into piles like stalagmites on the floor of a cave and your cupboards are almost bare, now, as you make definite plans for the weekend, remember to reserve some of this time for play. You have two tasks for Friday. The first is to conclude the week's work. The second is to start awakening your Wild Woman.

Friday's Meaning

The Nordic Goddess of love and fertility, Freya, gave us the name for Friday. Wagner identifies her with Idunna, who gave the gods the fruit of immortality, the golden apples. She loves everything that is pleasurable, harmonious, beautiful. She loves jewels, clothes, lovemaking, and arts and crafts. What they don't tell you in Greek and Roman mythology is that she is also a warrior Goddess who had the right to choose half of the heroes who died on the battlefield and take them to Sess-rumnir, her many-seated hall. In the earliest myths, the gentle Goddess whose power made men and women come together to beget new life was also the one who harvested it at the end so that the cycle of life could continue.

Friday Is Love Day

On Friday refrain from chores and think only of beautiful, effortless things. Friday is Freya's day, dedicated to the northern Goddess of love. Freya, like Venus and Aphrodite, is a Goddess of beauty and feeling, although she, too, can be fierce and wild. The planet that rules this day is Venus, Lady of Love. It is not simply because this day begins the weekend that it is the traditional time for dating. The Goddess smiles on those who get together on her day.

The power of the planet Venus governs love and romance and the results of love, both literally and metaphorically. It promotes fertility and creativity. On this day, ask her blessing on all the work you have done during the week so that it may prosper and grow. Ask that the relaxation of the weekend inspire you, so that when Monday comes around again, a whole new batch of creative ideas will burst into flower. Venus especially affects artists and other creative workers, all those involved in the beauty and fashion industries, entertainment, music—everything that appeals to the esthetic sense and releases the feelings.

Get a newspaper and see if you can catch a play or a movie or dance on Friday evening. Plan to go hiking on the weekend. Invite friends to come with you who will add to your enjoyment. Stick to your original idea of what your relaxation time should be like and do not give up your plans because your friends want to stay home watching TV. A working woman is cooped up for so much of her life that she has to get aired out and renew herself spiritually.

The Goddess of Friday: Freya/Venus

Sometimes when you come out of the office at the end of the day you can see, glowing gently in the western sky, the evening star. You are looking at Venus (the Roman name for Freya), Lady of Love and the most enduring of Goddesses. She blesses your nights, but she can bless your days as well. Some say she is the oldest of Goddesses, second only to Earth herself, and perhaps it is true, for if Venus, whom the Greeks called

Aphrodite, did not bring male and female together, how could the other gods have been created, and how could life go on?

Some say Venus came originally from Asia Minor. In those days, she was a Goddess who could go to war if there was need. The Greeks tried to tame her, but the poets called her "awe-full gold-crowned, radiant Aphrodite" and feared her power. The singer of the *Carmina Burana* called Venus the world's illumination, rose of the world, at a time when Venus, like the rest of the old gods, was supposedly long gone. They say that her Scandinavian sister, Freya, was the last of the Norse deities to receive worship from men.

This should be no surprise. None of the new patriarchal religions has known how to deal with the power of sexual love. But Venus is more than a goddess of sexual passion. She is present in all the "tender" feelings. She was born from the sea foam, and it is her power you feel when the beauty of a song, a sunset, or a memory moves you to tears. She is not afraid to give way to emotion—your feelings are proof that you are still alive! All of the things that enable you to enjoy the world instead of just endure it are her gifts: pity, tenderness, grace, delight, romance, charm, and laughter.

Men pretend these gifts have no place in the working world, but they are helpless when the Goddess appears, not as a sex object but as a queen. When you bring the power of Venus into the workplace, the corporate jungle can become a garden.

Call upon the power of Venus on a Friday, when you need to bring harmony and graciousness to your working situation and, of course, if you are doing a love spell. Pray, like Sappho, "What my heart most hopes will happen, make happen; you yourself join forces on my side!"

Friday's Scent

Venus loves roses, but cedar and sandalwood, cypress and myrtle are her scents as well. The Bach remedy to escape all worries is agrimony. Try a few drops.

Friday's Gem

Friday's gem is the emerald, the gem of Venus.

Friday's Color

Friday's color is green. *Mint green* is calming. Green is the favorite color of nature; it heals the spirit. Green stimulates orientation toward the future and frees one from the past. It is also a money color; wear green and think green, and you may avoid being broke.

Apple green is a stimulating color. You accept challenges better when wearing this green. It helps you see new opportunities and perks up your interest in the world.

Moss green is the most subtle and nurturing color in the green spectrum. It is peaceful but strong and helps you maintain consistent energy. It is a supportive color, although in its darker shades it can convey an understated authority. The lighter and brighter tones, such as *avocado,* are more assertive and cheerful.

Primary (or grass) green stands out when you wear it in a drab office. It communicates ambition, health and vigor, independence, and calm emotions.

Blooms in the Office

Keep fresh-cut flowers or flowering live plants in the office. The flowers are current; they represent your here and now. Crystals have good effects on us, but flowers are as perishable as the moments of our lives. They mirror back our own transience and teach us to accept it gracefully. Each flower has a meaning and an emotional effect on the woman around it. And all flowers, whatever is in season, have a calming and uplifting effect on our feelings and self-esteem.

A single rose will say, "I love you." Marigolds, with their bold yellow heads, whisper, "You are powerful." Hydrangeas say that you are abundant, and orchids that you are delicate and precious. Violets say, "The fairies are with you." Jasmine tells you that you are special. Carnations will say that your beauty is enduring. Lilacs will whisper that love is on its way to you. The lily of the valley says that you have been noticed.

The meanings of flowers vary from culture to culture and from woman to woman. Listen to the flowers when you step into a flower shop and pick the ones that speak to you. Flowers are the friends of your feelings. Instead of leaving your feelings at the door, give them company with flowers.

Grow green plants in pots if you can. They can make oxygen and remind you of the wild things. If you have sun in your window, geraniums will grow. They are magical flowers that bloom the year round, require little care, and stand for prosperity and financial success. If you cannot trust yourself to keep anything alive in your office but have at least a little sun, try air plants. All you have to do is spray them with water every so often. Air plants are a marvelous life form, needing no earth to grow. The plant hangs in there with you in your high-rise with a minimum of support. Air plants can even bloom and astonish you with their beauty.

Spell Work for Friday

1. Seven-Breath Spell Against Fear

If fear grips you, and you must shake it off immediately, get bergamot oil and put it on a small cotton ball. Hold it in your hand so it warms up a bit. Inhale its scent so deeply it reaches your toes and say:

>Fear be gone from my toes.

(Breathe into your legs as you inhale the scent of bergamot.)

>Fear be gone from my legs.

(As you continue banishing the fear, breathe the bergamot into the appropriate part of your body.)

Fear be gone from my hips.
Fear be gone from my heart.
Fear be gone from my throat.
Fear be gone from my mind.

By the time you finish, your mind will be filled with images of green things, growing and happy. Fear will lose its grip on you.

2. A Love Spell for the Office

It can happen.

You are falling in love with somebody at work—available or not. I am not going to talk you into or out of it; there is no use in doing that if the Wild Woman wants to get involved. The desire is growing. It starts interfering with your work. What are you going to do?

The Wild Woman has gotten you into trouble, no question about it. She is not going to rest until this attraction plays itself out. You probably wouldn't want someone who was forced to love you completely against his or her will, but you can certainly assist nature to take its course.

One thing you can do is to feed the person you love love foods. If you can bake, make some vanilla cookies (get a recipe from any cookbook) and put them out at coffee break (that communal coffee pot is a hotbed of magic), or give them to the loved one as a gift. While you bake, visualize this person loving you and saying romantic things to you, and also being honest and without bad habits. If you can't bake, buy the cookies ready-made and sprinkle them with vanilla powder as your spell. Season the cookies generously with vanilla bean.

You can buy this ground or grind it yourself. As you grind, you can whisper a spell over the beans (three times, of course).

> Warm seed, warm heart,
> May I and (name) never part.

The cookies can be shared with others in the office, just as long as your intended gets one. The place will be filled with the scent of vanilla, a most stimulating scent for sexual arousal. An aroused office can be a very happy office.

You can achieve the same purpose by cooking with coriander. Put the same spell on the coriander as on the vanilla bean and use it to spice the food you offer your intended.

3. Rune Spell for Getting What You Really Need

When you use the Germanic runes, the ancient European magical alphabet, you are using your right brain, because you are "writing weird." To do a rune spell, you need only to contemplate what you need and combine the runes required to attain it.

For this spell, you will be working with the rune Wunjo ᛈ. Wunjo is the rune of joy. When it appears, the scarcity has ended. It is now time to receive the blessings you have desired for so long. Now you can rejoice; the force of life has carried you across the hardships, and joyous new energy, light, and clarity are coming your way.

Make a nice big Wunjo, maybe with a green pen, and, as you do so, visualize the blessings you need. Take it outside under the new moon and breathe on it; then fold it toward yourself three times. Your breath is the breath of life, which this entity is now receiving, and in folding it toward yourself, you are gathering in the harvest.

Now tear the Wunjo into tiny pieces and scatter them to the four directions, thinking about how this entity is leaving you to become one with the universe. It will return to you the blessings that you envisioned while drawing Wunjo on the paper. Say

> Wunjo, Wunjo, rune of joy,
> Gather for me the satisfaction,
> Gather for me the blessings I need.
> According to my word, so mote it be!

During the day make it a mental habit to tell yourself, "All my needs are easily met." Take a moment to visualize your needs being filled; then let go of the problem and go back to work. Do a separate spell for each separate need. Do only one at a time, preferably at the new moon.

4. Vision Quest

In the workshops I teach, we spend a weekend together in some beautifully appointed campground, possibly during the full moon. In such a place you have a chance to really leave the office behind, to fill your lungs with fresh air, your ears with bird song, and your eyes with the vast expanse of the universe. Being in the wilderness is like a tonic for your soul. You start relaxing and listening within.

The Friday night session is for introductions and an opening circle in which we chant together and experience our collective energy. On Saturday we hike into the wilderness, pausing at great trees, lakes, or springs, and make a ritual of purification, blessing each other with water and swimming if we can. We eat great vegetarian meals. At night we worship the Goddess in our circles, the full moon being her visible manifestation. Here we practice using our right brain, praying and chanting again, raising our energy on each other's behalf, as we say aloud what we need in our lives, lighting candles on a natural altar. I use a lot of movement in this work, always involving the woman from head to toe in the spiritual quest.

Wild Woman enjoys dreaming. She appreciates expanding her consciousness, but after a while she will get restless, and then her mind wants special gourmet food to absorb in the form of specially designed experiences.

Sundays we go on vision quests, each on our own or in a group without speaking. Silence is a great solace. Inner voices can be heard more loudly and clearly when we stop the chatter. Sunday night we perform a closing circle and return to our lives, with our psychic batteries recharged.

There are many variations on this plan. Guided meditations or trance work can take you to visit the dead; meet angels; reexperience your past lives; make friends with wolves, deer, bears, and snakes as your totem animals; or ask questions of nature and have nature give you a special answer. When you are connecting all your powers, your soul is well nourished. You are no longer a spiritual orphan.

The Vision Quest Spell

Do this at home on Friday when you begin your weekend. Prepare a bowl of special water. Float some marjoram from your spice rack in the bowl. Take a bath or a good long shower; then light a white candle and stand on the floor naked with a little bit of salt sprinkled underneath your feet.

Look deeply into the bowl of water and breathe over it seven times for the moon. Then say:

> This is the life-giving water of the universe.
> It flows within me and outside of me.

(Now think about your feelings.)
Then say:

> I shall be renewed as the earth is renewed by the rain.
> I shall be cleansed as the earth is cleansed by the rain.

(Now think about the water as your blood.)
Then say:

> This is the precious blood of the Mother Earth.
> In her I am healed; in her I am redeemed.
> In her I am made whole.

(Now drink some of this water, and, as you drink it, think of the words you have spoken and what water means to you and all life. Let the liquid slowly go down your throat.)

Finally, say:

> I am open to my own inner voice.
> I am healed by her presence within me.
> Blessed be. It is done. It is done. It is done.

Dress now and resume your normal activities. Pour the rest of the water out on a plant. If you felt anxious, obsessing, agitated emotions, inhale marjoram from the crushed fresh herb, and it will comfort you. As the weekend goes on, you will experience energy and feel new interest rise within you. You will do unexpected things you didn't plan on doing.

Friday Meditation: Wild Woman Gets Ready for the Weekend

On Friday night, take a purifying bath with some bath salts or herbal oils. Then lie down in a safe place where you can relax and meditate on your Wild Woman. Go see her in her favorite safe place, in the woods, and ask her what she will need to do to feel stronger this weekend. Watch her move for you, make her sounds, even ask her to point to parts of the body that need attention.

I usually see her waiting for me on a bench under the trees. She is rocking herself back and forth, a method she uses to relax and comfort herself. When I ask her to embrace me, she presses her furry body against mine with such wild longing that I know she needs to be touched. She has been short on human contact lately. When I ask her what she needs, she looks at me with those soulful wild eyes and opens her mouth for a wild howl. To me, this means she is lonely. She needs sex. She needs a party, or, better yet, a celebration with other Wild Women or Wild Men outdoors. How about a midnight picnic?

If you have an emotional support group, gather on a Friday night and talk about your lives. Eat, drink, and feel the priceless sense of belonging to one's own tribe. The Wild Woman must have a tribe. She needs more than one friend and one lover. If you are isolated, this is a good time to visit women's bookstores. Check out their bulletin boards and leave little notes calling other women to form a Wild Woman group to grow and nurture each other. You can tie in to other women through Goddess publications or feminist magazines. The helping hand is often at the end of your own wrist.

Light candles around your house and be a witch on Friday. Cast spells; make the spiritual connection to your roots as a woman of power. Read my other books, *Grandmother of Time, Grandmother Moon,* and *The Holy Book of Women's Mysteries.*

Friday is a good night to take care of your body and soul.

Saturday

A Day for Visioning

Saturday's Energy

The long-awaited weekend is here! On Saturday you can sleep in, nest and rest, and do pleasurable things. Today you don't have to go to the office, and yet the way you use your days off may make all the difference to your work and daily life. On Saturday, allow your mind to expand. Expose your brain to new experiences, read books, go outdoors to think and meditate, attend a weekend workshop, give a party, or create personal rituals.

Saturday's Naming

Saturday is named after the planet Saturn. We are used to thinking of Saturn as Father Time, the god of old age and decay, and although you may feel like him by the time the weekend rolls around, this is not the way the ancients looked at Saturn. In the old days, age and maturity were honored.

Saturnus ruled the world during the proverbial Golden Age. In ancient Rome, the Winter Solstice (December 21) was marked by the celebration of Saturnalia, a festival that tried to recreate the golden time before civilization. During the Golden Age, everybody was equal. There were no slaves and no masters, no subordinate or superior sexes, no tyrants or landlords.

Saturn himself was Old Man Winter, crowned with evergreens, drinking his foamy ale as his decorated chariot was pulled through the streets of the city. He and his good wife, Ops, the Goddess of plenty and good fortune from whose name the word "opulence" comes, brought winter cheer into the villages of old Italy. Revels were held with dances, masks were donned, and the rules of restrictive social behavior such as the separation of the classes were suspended. Women and men enjoyed themselves freely on the streets and feared none. All we have left to remind us of this Golden Age today are a few days of Mardi Gras in New Orleans and the greater celebration in Brazil.

Saturn's day, when you are your own boss, is a good time to imagine alternative realities.

Saturday's Goddess: Athena Invents the World

Athena is the true Goddess for the working world, because she invented the wheel and all arts and sciences. Athena, who according to Robert Graves originated in Africa, invented weaving, civil law, sewer systems, land irrigation, and the arts of strategy and defense. She wields the thunderbolt—the power of electricity, which is everything the office runs on. You have cars to go to work in; you have wheels of trains and the wheels in the office; even the computers are under her rule because they run on the electric signals Athena rules today.

Turn to Athena when you need energy to finish important projects, when you need to practice power, when you need to have a winning strategy, when you are fighting for your own defense. Athena encourages women in their studies, helps them achieve professional advancement, even helps in childbirth. Her symbol is the olive branch, the universal sign of peace.

You can access Athena energy by focusing on her image, a strong black woman dressed in a long, flowing chiton, with a shimmering, white silken mantle with purple trimmings around her shoulders. She wears a helmet on her head. The helmet symbolizes her mind protection—Athena is no fool. It will remind you to cultivate watchfulness of the mind and preparedness. Her sacred bird is the owl, whose meaning is wisdom. Owls are the allies of farmers because they get rid of vermin. Pictures of owls in your office assure you of Athena's presence. Altars to her are decorated with olive branches, blue candles, and amber incense. A single spray of olive branch could count as her altar.

When you need help to gain vision, a promotion, or protection at the workplace, meditate on Athena and her powers of wit and wisdom. Light a little amber incense or any other kind you enjoy, imagine her mighty image in your mind, and say·

Athena is my strength.
She is my armor.
I walk in peace and safety.
Her shield deflects all harmful.

With Athena behind you, be bold and go after your dreams.

Saturday's Scent

Spend the day scent-free and get to know your own body's scent. In the evening, if you are going out, dab on a little oil of amber.

Saturday's Gems

The gem of friendship is *tiger's eye*. *Amber,* known as the symbol of the Sun Goddess, is great for happiness and healing.

Saturday's Color

Security and stability are the message to us from the color *brown,* the color of the good earth. Brown calms down excessive mental activity and puts you in touch with your body. It is a good grounding color. You are never seen as threatening while wearing brown.

Gray neutralizes outside stress, prevents too much involvement, and communicates a self-protective image. "This is a passive and calm person" is the message of this color. If you are seen as a threatening personality, wear gray, and a lot of people will relax and change their minds. For this reason gray can be used to temper the effects of black. Wear white and yellow as a follow-up, so that you aren't perceived as too colorless, but keep something gray handy just in case the old ugly resentment against you rises again.

Saturday's Woman: Visions of a Golden Age

True vision may be the most important tool for making global and personal history. Think back to the fifteenth century and Joan of Arc. A simple peasant girl had a vision of France becoming a free and unified country. For years, France had been at the mercy of the English, who controlled half the country. Joan's vision infused others with a sense of missionary zeal and made soldiers out of mercenaries, drove the English army out of her country, and crowned a king, all before she was nineteen! Of course, men found her success disturbing, and finally both sides betrayed her. A Frenchman captured her and sold her to the English, who accused her of witchcraft because she had worn men's clothes and led armies to victory. Refusing to deny her vision, she was burned at the stake.

But the French people did not forget Joan of Arc, and eventually the church leaders canonized her as a saint. Joan's mother even sued the new state of France and collected damages for the loss of her daughter. Soon statues and images of the virgin warrior, a young woman fighting for the good of all, became part of the French identity.

Joan of Arc derived her spiritual power from her inner life, from her prayers and the visions she saw and the voices she heard. Vision is powerful. What is your vision? How can you manifest it at work and play? Can you revolutionize your company? Take risks; take charge. Let your zeal be known at the office. Learn to lead.

Spells for Saturday Visions

1. Prophetic Dreams

After you have expanded your mind by reading your favorite women visionaries' works and exploring the possibilities other women have envisioned, use a dream pillow made of artemisia and mints to stimulate your own deep mind to visualize the plan for your life. Keep this pillow on your bed so you can smell the herbs all night long. *Artemisia vulgaris,* or *mugwort,* is known to release prophetic dreams to the dreamer. A good time to use your dream pillow is on Friday night, so that on Saturday morning, when you can sleep in, you have more time to try to remember your dreams.

Keep a journal at your bedside and jot down your dreams. When you discover a theme, follow it up. If you are dreaming about a lot of trees, plant a tree. If you have escaping dreams in which you are running away from something, try to confront your pursuer next time and see what this fear actually is. If somebody is trying to hurt you in a dream, you can say, "I bless you and release you!" This makes the frightening image change and perhaps tell you what it wanted all along.

Lucid dreaming is a state in which you know you are dreaming and have some control over what is going on. Get into a state in which images emerge naturally into your awareness and play with them. Call forth things you are usually too scared to face, for example, your dead relatives, and ask them to talk to you. See if your ancestors are at peace or not. See if your ancestors will help you with insights.

Before bedtime you can sip saffron tea to improve your dreaming. A bath with lavender scent relaxes the body and the mind.

2. Acting on Your Dreams

Dreaming is just the beginning. The mother of wisdom is action. Once a step is taken, it gives birth to the next step. Keep making those steps and don't lose your own identity. Translating your dreams into reality is true witchcraft. It is bending reality, transforming life, being the creator. When you gain a vision of importance, the whole world will benefit. Women now more then ever must envision the future, or there won't be any.

119

3. Raising Consciousness: Fun, Empowering, Weekend Work

Consciousness is the power tool of vision. A raised consciousness is the tool that will allow you to survive the last death spasms of patriarchy. Consciousness is self-knowledge and self-loyalty and self-love, rooted in the cosmic conviction that we are all one. We are all connected. Everything that happens to any individual woman is actually happening to the entire female group soul. Consciousness is the door through which we must walk out into the future. Women need the company of other women in order to strengthen their own female identities.

4. Bach Flower Essence Remedy for Finding a Sense of Purpose

If you think it's too late for you, and you cannot see any purpose in your life and have given up on finding your life work, try this. Take a few drops of *wild oats* to heal your subtle, emotional body. Taking this essence will help you to define your calling in life and to clarify your mind about who you are and what you are here for.

5. Vision Mandala

One of the best ways to actualize your visions is to make a picture of them. This doesn't necessarily require you to be an artist. If you have a scissors and some paste, you can manifest your vision through a collage. Collect magazines with pictures of things you want to bring into your life and, when you have a fair number, buy a big piece of posterboard at an art store. You can make a collage simply by pasting pictures together in a way that pleases you, or you can construct it in the form of a mandala.

To make a mandala, draw a large circle the width of the posterboard. The circle can be divided concentrically or in radiating sections. One approach is to divide it into seven sections, one for each of the powers discussed in this book. In the center of the mandala, paste a photo of yourself. If the purpose of this mandala is to manifest certain qualities in your career, in the photo you should be wearing business clothes.

Radiating outward from your picture, combine pictures that portray or symbolize the ways in which you would like to manifest each power in your life. For instance, in the survival section, you might include pictures of people eating good food, or mighty mountains, a fertile garden, the kind of house you would like to live in, images of the Mother Goddess, female athletes, and the like. For will, you could put together photos of women in leadership positions, pictures of things you feel passionate about, newspaper headlines, a lioness or some other powerful female animal, and the like. You can also add appropriate printed materials from the office—a pay stub, a memo of praise, a position posting for which you would like to apply.

You can use felt pens or crayons to add color and enhance and connect the pasted materials, to write in slogans, affirmations, titles, definitions, and the like. Look at pictures of medieval stained-glass windows and Tibetan mandalas for ideas on how these design elements can be combined. When you are done, you can shellac the whole thing and frame it. Hang it in your bedroom or over a table you are using as an altar. Every time you look at it, you will be reminded of the person you have envisioned yourself becoming. This then acts like a daily spell on your mind, calling in the desired events one by one.

Saturday's Meditation: Wild Woman Meets the Ancestors

You are the last green leaf on your own tree of life. Your ancestors are the trunk and the roots and other branches from which you have budded. The last green leaf depends on the rest of the tree to nourish it, but it is the leaves that send the living energy of the sun to the rest of the tree. In the same way, your ancestors depend on you to keep their memory alive with your energy.

In Western culture we have forgotten this and bury and forget our dead, but Wild Woman remembers. Even Halloween, which was originally intended to celebrate and remember the dead, has become no more than a time of fun and games with costumes and pranks.

When well tended, our ancestors become our special guardian angels. For example, when my grandmother spoke my name as her last words, according to our family tradition she was signing up to be my special guardian. She saved my life during the Hungarian revolution and helped me escape from Hungary. Even today she comes to me as a distinct voice in my head when I am in dire need. I am very lucky to have a devoted grandmother on the other side.

How to Reach Your Ancestors

Relax your body as you have done in the other meditations by filling it with your own breath. Breathe into your toes and legs and hips and stomach and breasts and neck and face and brain. Each breath should be taken slowly and sensitively. When the last breath has cleared your lungs, imagine yourself in that safe forest where you usually find your Wild Woman.

This time dress in white and come with the thought that you will soon see your own ancestors on the other side. It is so reassuring to see them face to face. When you have done so, you will forever know that life and death are interconnected and that one is the opposite side of the other. For those who fear death, as we all do, this journey is a healing journey to the source of life.

Barefoot, follow a dirt path down to a valley, which you already sense is the land of the dead. Pick some flowers along the way and take note what kind of flowers come to your hands. Make them into a nice bouquet. The temperature will get colder and colder as you descend.

Moist fog rolls in, and you begin to see some shapes in the mist ahead of you. The mist prevents you from seeing who those shapes are, but as you walk boldly among them, call for the spirits of your own family to come and greet you.

Do not lose faith if they take their time in coming. After all, this is your first visit—did you expect them to be waiting?

But suddenly you know they are all there. Look into the face of the ancestor who seems most eager to talk to you. If you recognize her or him, say hello. If you don't, ask for a name and how you are related. Remember what your ancestor tells you. Now offer to the spirits the flowers you have picked, a few for each. Flowers are like breath; the dead get energy from them.

Now more faces come into view. Abide in this place until they do. Visit with them and don't be afraid. Tell them you love them—it will make them cheerful. Ask how they feel about you. Would they like to see you more often? If you have any questions about your family or yourself, this is a good time to ask one of the ancestors for answers. You would be surprised how glad they are to help the living.

Promise to make frequent visits to the beloved dead a part of your life. Create a special spot in your house where all their photographs can be displayed and their mementos gathered. Place some fruit and a glass of water by the photos; burn incense when you think about them. If you do this, dreams in which your ancestors appear will come more often, and you will constantly benefit from their advice and their unseen helping hands.

When you feel that you have gotten what you needed from this encounter, say goodbye to your relatives and start walking back up the dirt path. Climb to the very top of the mountain, where you imagine yourself turning into the wind, and fly back into your body on the wings of your own breath. Once back in your body, breathe into the top of your head, your neck, your shoulders and arms, your chest and stomach, then your hips, your legs, and wiggle your toes.

Make these visits at the time of the waning moon, when the spirits of the dead come nearer.

The results of this work can be dramatic. Once when we did this exercise in a workshop, a woman whose mother died in childbirth came face to face with her, and the woman knew immediately who she was. Her mother said to her, "I am always with you; I will always protect you." This woman stopped being an orphan right then and there because she had met her mother, and from then on she was able to visit with her mother every month. For others, the wisdom of the ancestors has provided insights into their own personalities, fates, and relationships.

For the Spirit

Sunday's Energy

Sunday is a time to celebrate the spirit—and the body as well. It is a time to cook fine meals, visit with friends, and hike in the woods or go to the beach, make phone calls or sleep all day.

Do not waste your weekend on chores. Don't give away the only chance you have to unwind for the sake of neatness and a reputation as a good housekeeper. The best use of your weekend is to open yourself to a new spiritual experience, which you will treasure for years to come. You can change your life over the weekend: take workshops and classes, do inner work along with outside work, integrate your body and soul.

Sunday's Name

Sunday is the day of the sun, with all its associations of power, vitality, self-expression, pride, creativity, and life. Traditionally

Sunday is connected to gold, judges, kings, and favor. It has been taken to mean the male principle of the universe, the power of male authority, but in mythology, especially the mythologies of northern Europe, the sun is just as often a Goddess. Its warmth is her love; its light, the richness of her robes; its gift, the plenty of the earth.

Sunday's Scent

Wear a citrus scent, such as *lemon* or *tangerine,* to honor the sun and make you feel fresh and vital.

Sunday's Gem

Gold, which has the color of the sun, is the gem for Sunday. If you have gold, wear it today.

Sundays' Colors

If you have been feeling like a workhorse lately, and too much stress is crowding your feelings out, if you need to relax your mind and listen to your heart or stimulate your own femininity, wear *pink*.

Wear *orange* when you need more energy to pull yourself up by the bootstraps, heal yourself from depression, recover from the flu or other illness, bring in desired results from projects, or organize and motivate yourself.

Knowing the Unseen

Knowledge is a distillation of information from the intuitive universe. This "knowing" is what we get from the universe; it appears in our minds and makes us create the corresponding thought forms without even trying. It is a kind of involuntary thinking, outside the realm of our control. Truth is usually glimpsed through this kind of knowing. We have only to look up or glance at the face of our beloved to suddenly "know" what he or she is unable to tell us. We know if we have chosen correctly; we know when we are on the right path and when we are hopelessly lost.

This ability to *know* can get rusty when no attention is paid to it. Returning to the sources of our inner lives is the cure for rusting souls.

A woman needs retreats where she can be quiet and listen within. She needs a space that is safe for her and yet creative, where she is not a caretaker but a receiver of care. She needs time for herself just to follow the rhythms of her own breathing or allow her mind to lose itself in meditation instead of in job-related anxiety, self-improvement, or trivia. She needs to get disconnected from her everyday worries, which are constantly changing, and get reconnected to the All-Mind, which is like a steady peaceful space where she can get a perspective on things.

Meditating

Psychic powers can be claimed when we use this faculty of knowing called *meditation*. There is no limit to the value of this ancient spiritual practice.

I recommend the *unfocused meditation* mode for women, *not* the one with a mantra that needs to be repeated endless times ad nauseam. Instead, I like to sit quietly and allow all my thoughts to simply flow by as if I were watching a movie. When you are meditating in this way, do not get involved with those thoughts, do not judge, and do not linger. Let the river of thoughts flow by. This is the way most natural to women.

Breathe consciously in and out and follow the rhythm of your own breath. This kind of free-flowing meditation relaxes the central nervous system and gives you a chance to tap into your sources of power. Meditate in this way for five, then ten, and then eventually twenty minutes each day.

Meditation is simply a way of shutting down the chattering conscious mind by some trick (be it repetition of words, chanting, or even sex) and letting the All-Mind and your own mind connect in peace. You can meditate alone in nature, unobserved, walking, hiking, and listening within. Your inner life, the life of the spirit, is the most exciting adventure of all.

Enlightenment and Psychic Powers

Creativity is a kind of meditation that pursues an inner discovery. In creating an art form, be it visual or musical, poetry or stories, we go to the same magical well to draw our material. Mysteries of the universe exist within us; we can become channels for universal wisdom. Creativity is the mother of invention, the origin of science and art. It promotes wholeness within the individual who is practicing it. Creativity benefits the entire human species. When the individual creates, the All-Mind gets nourishment back.

Transcendence has been held up to us modern people as the ultimate payoff for our soul's evolution. But whether you seek freedom from rebirth like the Hindus, dying on the cross with Jesus like the Christians, or flying through the night breeze like the witches, the place where you experience transcendence is between your two ears. Since transcendence is the ultimate experience, beyond words, I will not describe it. In my experience, this state has been achieved most often in improvised rituals that suddenly "take off."

Transcendence does not require that you give up your power to somebody else, turn over your livelihood to a sect, or give up your legal existence in the real world. It simply means that you perceive yourself being one with the One.

Enlightenment comes in a steady flow to all of us, every day. There are many degrees of enlightenment, from small sparks of insight to transcendent illuminations.

"Before enlightenment, drawing water and sweeping the corners, after enlightenment—drawing water and sweeping the corners," says an old Chinese proverb.

Before enlightenment you can be quite content, toeing the line and thinking that there is no better way to live. You may accept your lack of pleasure, lack of friends, and isolation because you think that is how it's supposed to be. Then you receive an aha! experience, become enlightened, and are able to see and understand your situation in the world. You see that the bad things that have happened to you are not your fault, you remember the sexual harassment and lack of equal rights, and you get mad. You may even long for your former unenlightened ignorance, but it is too late. In the universe of which you are a part, everything is constantly changing, including you. Resisting natural law is useless. Enlightenment comes, and with it a new set of challenges and feelings. Say goodbye to your old state of passivity and slavery. Goodbye addictions, goodbye misery.

Divining Your Future

Tarot cards are my favorite tools, but runes and the I Ching are great, and so are the many more exotic means—reading tea leaves or chicken bones, taking omens from the winds or birds—that people have invented to peer into the depths of the universe.

When I was starting out as a young witch, taking a look at

the cards was always helpful. "What's in the cards?" we would ask, and my mother would throw the Gypsy cards and get all kinds of specific messages from them. Her own fortuneteller, Magda, came weekly, and she was the first to detect my mother's breast cancer, which was then cured.

Pull a Tarot card and read its meaning for yourself for the day. The ideas suggested by the symbols will remind you of the ancient roots of your own All-Mind. You will gain access to a new vocabulary of the spirit. This will exercise your ability to go beyond the rational and travel in the realm of "irrational" wisdom as well. The Tarot is a book of symbols, which is the language of the spirit. Images work in a very important way. Our minds need images as they need words. Nonverbal insights are profound and desirable.

Going to See a Psychic Reader

Your own preparation will have a great effect on how good a reading you will receive when you go to see a psychic reader. I always ask my clients to write out their questions without any editing on a piece of paper and to bring it along. This writing helps to stir up your deep mind and make you think and feel deeply, like a lake when the bottom is stirred up.

Next, I ask my clients to recognize that what we are about to do is irrational. Allow the right brain to surface. When you select cards, pull them for *no* reason at all. Some people like to search for cards and pull them because they are hot or cold, they stick out, or they hide. Those are all reasons. Irrational means you pull the cards without worrying about why you are doing it. Only then can the deep mind come into play. Around the end of the reading I ask my client to take out the list of questions and check to see if anything has been left out. Usually all the person's concerns have been covered somehow.

As a psychic I can help you to face the different forces and currents in your life and advise you on how to ride them out while they last. Let's say you have felt very jumpy lately. You have been aware of an urge to end relationships, quit your job, move out of town. If the Tower turns up in your reading, we will know that these feelings are good (even if they feel bad at the time), that revolution is the current theme in your life, and that some of those impulses can have beneficial effects. Now isn't this a relief?

If you feel very ambitious and don't know why, and the Emperor turns up, I would advise you to seek more power and follow that ambition, because it's well accepted. If you are lonely, and I see the Empress coming in the near future, I would tell you to hang on, for soon a climate of love will enfold you, and then cruise, baby, cruise. I can tell you roughly what is going to happen at least three months ahead, sometimes a year. But I am not the force that makes these things come to pass. You are. It is your own fate that shows up in the cards. I am simply the one who holds the mirror and interprets the images.

There are some people whose sole talent is finding lost objects, or people who train themselves in this field—mostly Las Vegas–type performers. If you're looking for emotional support, you must find a support group on your own to sort out your feelings, or a good therapist.

Different kinds of psychics use different terminologies. In each area there are basic concepts that must be grasped before you can benefit at all. If you don't know how to use a psychic reader's work, tell her right away. She will have to explain more to you. Be specific. These ancient symbols don't have cards for modern jobs or situations, but they can indicate outcome.

Asking questions that can be answered by a "yes" or a "no" is usually most productive. There are also some things to watch out for. If a psychic tells you that you have had a curse put upon you by somebody and she needs so much money to remove it, watch out—you have just run into a well-known scam.

Spiritual counselors have a lot of power if you open yourself up to them. This is needed when you are getting spiritual healing but is an obstacle when you meet a charlatan. Choose your psychic with the same care you use to choose your physician. It is best to have a recommendation from somebody you know.

Your best source of counsel is your own spirit.

There are many ways to establish nonverbal communication with your own spirit. Go for a walk and, before you leave the house, ask yourself a question that is important to you. Then let go of the problem and take a nice walk in the woods, in the park, or on the seashore. Come back, and you will find that the answer has been formulated in your mind and that you understand it clearly.

Sunday's Goddess: Isis, Lady of Transitions

All women love Isis, the dark Madonna of Egypt. What an ancient blessing she is to us! Oldest of the old, they called her, old as the archetype for humanity, the gentle Madonna with her child assures us that we too are safe in her arms. Her image was used to portray Mary with her child, the Christian version of the Goddess.

Isis is the Queen of Heaven, Mother of all, protector of ships and life transitions. She is the one whose grace allows you to enter life, the one who waits at the end to receive you back into her open arms and cuddle you until it is time for the next lifetime. She is the one who performs the miracles of healing, the miracles of success and blooming, the miracles of fruiting and finally dying. She is known as the mother of rebirth.

Queen Isis, whose original name was Au Set—the seven lights of heaven—had sisterhoods of priestesses dedicated to her. These were the women who cared for her many shrines and dispensed her many miracles. Here the people could receive the medicines of healing, protection in childbirth, restoring sight to the blind, returning the use of arms and legs that were lame.

Isis was the Lady of the Words of Power who gained control over the proud sun god Ra by learning his secret name. Thoth the scribe taught her magic spells, but she was the one who put them to use in the world. By her magic she restored enough life to her slain husband to conceive a child.

Most enduring of the goddesses of Egypt, Isis's worship was carried throughout the Mediterranean by traders. There was a temple of Isis in Roman Londinium. Apuleius wrote about his devotion to her in *The Golden Ass*. She continues to be a major goddess for those who work with women's spirituality today.

A Theban inscription from the fourteenth century B.C. tells us:

In the beginning there was Isis:
Oldest of the old, she was the Goddess
from whom all becoming arose.
She was the Great Lady, Mistress of the two lands of
    Egypt,
Mistress of Shelter, Mistress of Heaven,
Mistress of the House of Life,
Mistress of the Word of God.
She was the unique.
In all her great and wonderful works, she was a wiser
    magician and more excellent than any other god.

Isis is the Goddess who could be called upon to end racism in the office. For example, if you have problems with racist remarks, put a picture of the Black Madonna on your wall and see how words and feelings will calm down.

Prepare an amulet of Isis thusly:

Obtain seven figs and a red cord, which you tie in a knot like an ankh, with only one loop, not two. Now place the seven figs in a bowl with water in it with these words:

Holy blood of Au Set,
Holy splendor of Au Set,
Holy magic power of Au Set,
Please protect the wearer of this amulet
And halt those who would harm me.

Let the cord steep in the water for seven minutes. Then take it out and, once it has dried, put it in your purse or pocket.

Eat the seven figs in honor of Isis. Pour the water onto your plants in the office or use it to purify the office by sprinkling it about.

Spells for Inner Knowledge

1. Spirit Carrying Your Body

You may be thinking that this is all very inspiring, but how can this weird power help in the office? It is true that unless you are a professional psychic, overt use of spiritual powers is not in commercial demand. But there are a number of things you can do to make the job you are being paid for easier.

This is another opportunity to let your Wild Woman get out and rule. When you go to work, carry your bones on your spirit spine. Mentally hang all your weight on your spirit body and ask your spirit to hold you up. Visualize this ethereal, luminescent body gently easing your material body onto her weightless shoulders, even slipping into it like a well-fitting glove. The spirit body is not accustomed to being in your body this much—she may want to split, slipping away into some fantasyland. However, for a set span of time, let's say ten minutes a day, try this mental exercise.

When your spirit body is carrying you, there will be a positive difference in the way you walk and sit and move your body. You will not tilt your neck and upper body forward as your body drags your spirit behind. Exercise your spirit in tangible, immediate ways. Eventually you will be able to do this all day long. At intervals, ask yourself, "Who is carrying me?" and see your own luminescent body glowing and radiating health and vigor from within.

2. A Bach Remedy to Strengthen Psychic Powers

A few drops of essence of *olive* taken daily promotes regeneration and restores balance. It helps you feel the peace of the Goddess, the serenity and openness that are important for the growth of the seventh power.

3. Rune Spell to Integrate Mind and Body

If you want to dream a solution to your problems by integrating mind and body, before you go to sleep draw upon the crown of your head the following runes. Say:

Berkano ᛒ for my body, Ansuz ᚨ for my mind, Kaunaz ᚲ for my passion, Fehu ᚠ for fertility of spirit.

Visualize each rune as you draw and say it, and then sleep peacefully.

4. Spirit Diet

I know a woman professor in biochemistry at Florida University who went on a *crystal diet*. She would let her crystal pendant swing above the food she was looking at in the market and ask her spirit if she should eat it. Depending on whether the crystal swung left or right, she knew whether a food choice was right or wrong for her. So she bought, cooked, and ate whatever the crystal directed her to. Eating like this, she lost sixty pounds. Did the crystal know? Or was her own inner guide using this opportunity to communicate her own deep wisdom about her needs?

The emotional payoff of this union with one's own spirit is the state of happiness that results from the constant interplay of the spheres, the divine dialogue. If you get so familiar with your spirit power that you can touch her at will, you will never feel alone again. You are already "mated" with your inner spirit. Be friends with your spirit; feed her what she wants to eat; let her carry your weight; let her choose foods for you and feed you back. When your reality includes spirit, you are involved in the divine union of the creator and the created, the ultimate cosmic meeting.

You already listen to your spirit in many ways. When you walk on the streets, you sense danger, you can sense if something is wrong. But you have been trained not to trust your own eyes, senses, and instincts. You have been told not to trust yourself when you are using your "woman's intuition." In order to hear your spirit loud and clear, you must retrain yourself. Get a pack of Tarot cards and a good book on the subject. Make a set of runes. Practicing divination is a good way to get your conscious mind talking to your deep soul. Re-claim your divine powers.

5. *Invoking Inspiration*

Spells are exercises through which we connect with the All-Mind. When alone or with sympathetic co-workers, begin a project by ringing a bell or bells. I use two small ones that I ring together above my head over my brains, and then behind me, over my shoulders and wherever feels right. I ring the bells to raise my own enthusiasm and alert my intuition. The sound wakes up the right brain and the left; it is like a herald saying, "Now we begin!" When you have finished the project, ring the bells joyously again to signify your achievement.

Light a purple candle with the name of the project written on it three times and burn the candle a few minutes each night for seven nights in a row. Each time, remember that the spirit within you is the kin to the great spirit outside of you, and that all you desire is fine with the universe.

You can improvise the words you say at candle-burning times. There is no holy book that tells us the right or wrong words. In every Earth religion you will find the awareness that the pure desire of the heart is the best prayer.

6. *Earth-Conscious Earning*

Be tuned in when you spend your hard-earned dollars. Who are you supporting with your money? Develop ways to shop that contribute to the survival of the earth instead of depleting it. Consumerism is pushed on us by companies that count on our gullibility and neediness. If your soul and emotional body are in order, you will not buy stuff that you don't need, clothes that you won't wear, food that will hurt you.

You create the economic future when you spend your money. Shopping is communication with the economy of the United States. Manufacturers need your support, so support those that help you with your needs. Boycott products whose manufacturers spend their money against women's rights. Read labels, however small the print, and let the industry know that you have had it with their torture of animals to develop a nail polish, with irradiating or spraying pesticides on your food, making your fruit look good but deadly to eat. Let them know you are not in the market for furs that require the killing of the wildlife around you. Most of all, let them know you are not voting for male or female candidates who take away your reproductive rights. Casting your vote at election times is a very effective way to communicate with the collective consciousness.

Let the world know your needs, and demand that it serve you well as a consumer and citizen. Power and happiness becomes you, my most regarded one; be blessed as you cross over to the twenty-first century.

Resources

Aswynn, Freyja. *Leaves of Yggdrasil.* St. Paul, MN: Llewellyn, 1990. (Female-centered runes.)

Bach, Edward. *Bach Flower Remedies.* New Canaan, CT: Keats, 1979.

Booss, Claire. *Scandinavian Folk and Fairy Tales.* New York: Avenel Books, 1984.

Budapest, Zsuzsanna E. *The Holy Book of Women's Mysteries.* Oakland, CA: Wingbow, 1989.

———. *The Grandmother of Time.* San Francisco: Harper San Francisco, 1989.

———. *Grandmother Moon.* San Francisco: Harper San Francisco, 1991.

Cunningham, Scott. *Magical Aroma Therapy.* St. Paul, MN: Llewellyn New Times, 1982.

———. *The Magic in Food.* St. Paul, MN: Llewellyn Publications, 1990.

———. *Encyclopedia of Magical Herbs.* St. Paul, MN: Llewellyn, 1991.

Don, Frank. *Color Magic.* Rochester, VT: Destiny Books, 1987. (Colors are powerful agents of making feelings.)

Emily's List. 1112 16th Street, N.W., Suite 750, Washington, DC 20036. (This is the place to send in your checks to help elect pro-choice women into the senate and congress. Do it!)

Faludi, Susan. *Backlash.* New York: Crown Publishing, 1992. (Powerful point of view, a must for psychic/political self-defense.)

Gardner, Kay. *Inner Landscape.* Stonington, ME: Caduceus Publications, 1990. (How sounds affect our bodies.)

Geuber, Richard, MD. *Vibrational Medicine.* Santa Fe, NM: Bear and Co., 1988.

Gleason, Judith. *Oya: In Praise of an African Goddess.* San Francisco: Harper San Francisco, 1992.

Monoghan, Patricia. *The Book of Goddesses and Heroines.* New York: Dutton, 1981. (Comprehensive and accurate.)

National Women's History Project. 7738 Bell Rd., Windsor, CA: 95492-8518. (Resource center for knowledge about our past, women in history, films, videos, teaching aids, slides, etc.)

The Original Swiss Arometics. P.O. Box 606, San Rafael, CA 94915. (Send to them for brochure of essences that are real.)

Potts, Bille. *Witches Heal.* Ann Arbor, MI: De Reve Publications, 1989. (Lesbian-centered healing with herbs.)

Scheffer, Mechtchild. *Bach Flower Therapy.* Rochester, VT: Healing Arts Press, 1979. (This is the Bible of Bach remedies.)

Stein, Diane. *The Natural Remedy Book for Women.* Freedom, CA: Crossing Press, 1992.

Stone, Merlin. *Ancient Mirrors of Womanhood.* Boston: Beacon Press, 1979. (A classic work of getting to know the Goddess from around the world.)

Teish, Luisah. *Jambalaya.* San Francisco: Harper San Francisco, 1985.

Warrig, Marilyn. *If Women Counted.* New York: Harper & Row, 1990. (What it means to be female financially.)

Weed, Susan S. *Healing Wise.* Woodstock, NY: Ash Tree Publishing, 1989. (Comprehensive herbal knowledge for healings.)

Wolf, Naomi. *The Beauty Myth.* New York: Morrow Publishing, 1991. (Good consciousness-raising material!)

Women of Power. P.O. Box 827, Cambridge, MA 02238. (Magazine of current goddess movement.)

About the Author

I was born in Budapest on January 30, 1940, on a terrible north-wind-whipped morning. My mother, Masika, then only twenty-five years old, had great trouble delivering me, so I was born by cesarean section. Mother was a famous sculptor who also happened to be a psychic, medium, and palm reader. She came from a long line of witches in the herbalist tradition. Her sister continued the line, becoming a pharmacist.

The Hungarian revolution in 1956 changed my life. I escaped to the West and went to school in Innsbruck and Vienna, and later at the University of Chicago, studying languages. I married and had two sons.

I studied with Second City, then with Viola Spolin, the mother of improvisation, and later at American Academy of Dramatic Art in New York.

In 1970 I discovered the Women's Liberation Movement, which led to another huge change in my life: I became a conscious woman. Feminism gave me so much. I decided to contribute seriously by connecting witchcraft with feminism, thereby sparking the women's spirituality movement. I wrote the first feminist witchcraft book, *The Feminist Book of Lights and Shadows,* which later became *The Holy Book of Women's Mysteries;* I followed this with two other books, *Grandmother of Time* and *Grandmother Moon.*

When I am not working on a new book I like to work with women at weekend workshops, retreats, and witch camps, where we practice the remembered arts of witchcraft in safe circles of women. We use tools of dance and chanting, candles, and incense to lift our spirits. We take part in guided meditations and pay visits to our ancestors and the Wild Woman. We practice using aromas and Bach remedies for inner balance.

Goddess in the Office workshops can be scheduled in your area. If you are a workshop producer or would like to be on my mailing list, write to the following address and I will let you know about developing programs: P.O. Box 11363, Oakland, CA 94611. Be sure to include your name and address.